Praise for
ALWAYS REMEMBERING

"The late, great Khenpo Jigme Phuntsok was a formidable figure in revitalizing Tibetan culture and monastic scholasticism in the wake of the Cultural Revolution—as much a visionary master of esoteric teachings as a champion of animal rights and religious tolerance. *Always Remembering* showcases a full range of his concerns: from foundational advice on Buddhist ethics to the history of Larung Gar, the ecumenical Buddhist academy he established in the 1980s. Thanks to Khenpo Sodargye's impetus in translating these and other gems of advice, his distinctive voice is reaching an ever-growing circle of Chinese- and English-speaking audiences."

—Holly Gayley, associate professor,
University of Colorado, Boulder

"*Always Remembering* offers an illuminating glimpse of the wisdom of Jigme Phuntsok Rinpoché grounded in the nomadic grasslands of eastern Tibet, reminding us of impermanence with poetic elegance, inspiring us to diligently seek out spiritual instruction, and advising us how to conduct ourselves virtuously in daily life."

—Sarah Jacoby,
Northwestern University

Kyabjé Jigme Phuntsok Rinpoché meeting disciples at his residence on the top of the great assembly hall at Larung Gar, late 1990s.

Always Remembering

Heartfelt Advice for Your Entire Life

His Holiness Jigme Phuntsok

Translated by Khenpo Sodargye

In Memory of the Thirteenth Anniversary of

Kyabjé Wish-Fulfilling Jewel's Parinirvana

Wisdom

Wisdom Publications
199 Elm Street
Somerville, MA 02144 USA
wisdompubs.org

Library of Congress Cataloging-in-Publication Data
Names: 'Jigs-med-phun-tshogs-'byuṅ-gnas, 1933–2004, author. |
Suodaji, Kanbu, 1962– translator.
Title: Always remembering: heartfelt advice for your entire life in memory of the thirteenth anniversary of Kyabjé wish-fulfilling jewel's parinirvana / translated by Khenpo Sodargye.
Description: Somerville, MA: Wisdom Publications, 2019. |
Includes bibliographical references. |
Identifiers: LCCN 2018040475 (print) | LCCN 2018061400 (ebook) |
ISBN 9781614296041 (ebook) | ISBN 9781614295808 (pbk.: alk. paper)
Subjects: LCSH: Rnying-ma-pa (Sect)
Classification: LCC BQ7662.2 (ebook) | LCC BQ7662.2 .J54 2019 (print) |
DDC 294.3/923—dc23
LC record available at https://lccn.loc.gov/2018040475

ISBN 978-1-61429-580-8 ebook ISBN 978-1-61429-604-1

23 22 21 20 19 5 4 3 2 1

Translated by Ke Jiang. Cover design by James Zaccaria. Interior design by Tony Lulek. Set in DGP 11 pt./15 pt. Photos on pages ii, 87, 117, and 126 courtesy of Larung Gar. Quotations from Shantideva courtesy of the Library of Tibetan Works and Archives.

Wisdom Publications' books are printed on acid-free paper and meet the guidelines for permanence and durability of the Production Guidelines for Book Longevity of the Council on Library Resources.

♻ This book was produced with environmental mindfulness. For more information, please visit wisdompubs.org/wisdom-environment.

Printed in the United States of America.

MIX
Paper from responsible sources
FSC® C011935

Please visit fscus.org.

Contents

Part 1. Poems

Part 2. Teachings

Preface

In 1933, out of his compassionate aspirations, a noble being came to this human world and remained until 2004. This noble being is the protector of sentient beings in the time of degeneration and our unsurpassable loving guru, Kyabjé Wish-Fulfilling Jewel (Jigme Puntsok Rinpoché).

In 2017, in memory of his passing away thirteen years earlier, the preparation committee of the Thirteenth Parinirvana Dharma Gathering of Kyabjé Wish-Fulfilling Jewel compiled a memorial book based on the transcriptions of some old audio recordings of our guru's teachings. The book falls into thirteen chapters, denoting the thirteenth anniversary of Kyabjé's parinirvana, and has seventy-one sections, indicating the number of years of his living in this world.

This slender book has extraordinary connotation and dependent origination. At the time, however, many Chinese followers felt sad for not being able to understand the contents because of the language barrier. As it turned out, due to special reasons my overseas lecture tour was cancelled and I was able to use this time to translate the book into Chinese. By doing so, I hoped more people, not having seen Kyabjé in person, would be able to connect with him through the Dharma.

Right afterward, I considered Kyabjé's aspiration when visiting Mount Wutai in 1987 that it would be best to guide all sentient beings on this planet onto the path of liberation. It is indeed true that in recent years, while lecturing in Europe and North America, I noticed the enthusiasm of many Westerners to learn about Tibetan Buddhism in general and about life and study at Larung Gar specifically. Hence the variety of topics in this book—including the lives and studies of Sangha members, the four great Dharma gatherings at Larung Gar, genuine and pretended tulkus from Tibet, and Tibetan culture and customs—provide readers with an immediate and direct experience of Tibetan Buddhism. In addition, Kyabjé's heartfelt advice on how to improve interpersonal relationships is a spiritual treasure to make you and me live with more ease and joy. Based on these thoughts and considerations, this English edition has come into being. I have done my best to be faithful to Kyabjé's simple and even manner of expression so that his words remain vivid and the feeling is created of listening to him directly. Only minor alterations of the subtitles in each chapter were made for clarity.

The Tibetan title was *Sporadical Instructions*. In order to remind readers to engrave these precious instructions, so rare and hard to encounter, in their hearts, I gave the title *Always Remembering* to this new English edition for Wisdom Publications, which is based on the Chinese translation. We remember the extraordinary range of our beloved guru's teachings by including five poems by Kyabjé as the first part of this English edition. The poems reveal Kyabjé's own devotion to his guru and inspire us even further in our determination to practice the genuine Dharma, to be free, and to work diligently for the liberation of all beings.

The first and foremost requirement of knowing a guru is to listen to his instructions. So this memorial book is extremely precious for every one of us. Just a word or two in it may play an inestimable role in your life and promote your liberation. If you carefully savor the seemingly plain words, you will find that the principles embedded in them are wondrously profound.

Through all the forms of our loving guru's teachings, may those fortunate ones be free from confusion and set foot on the path of liberation!

Sodargye
Larung Gar, Sêrtar

Written on this fourteenth day of the month of miracles in the earth-dog year of the seventeenth cycle (March 1, 2018).

Transliteration

Transliterated Sanskrit with full diacritics is used throughout the book. Phonetic Tibetan is used for terms that are in common usage in English (e.g., bodhichitta, nirvana, sadhana, samsara, sutra, Theravada, and so on).

Part 1.

Poems

ཧྲཱིཿ རཚེ་འདིའི་སྣང་ཚུལ་ལ་སྐྱོ་བའི་གླུ་ནགས་ཚལ་བུ་མོའི་དབྱངས་སྙན་ཞེས་བྱ་བ་བཞུགས་སོ།།

༡

ཧྲཱིཿ རྒྱལ་ཀུན་མཁྱེན་པའི་རང་གཟུགས་བཤེས་གཉེན་དུ་སྣང་བ།།
གཟུངས་སྤོབས་ཡོན་ཏན་བྱེ་བའི་གཏེར་མཛོད་ཀྱི་བདག་པོ།།
རིགས་བརྒྱའི་སྤྲོ་གཞི་མི་ཕམ་བློ་གྲོས་ནི་དྲི་མེད།།
འབྲལ་མེད་སྙིང་དབུས་པདྨོར་དགྱེས་བཞིན་དུ་བཞུགས་ཤིག །

༢

འདི་སྣང་བདེ་འབྱོར་རྨི་ལམ་ལྟ་བུ་ཡི་ཆོས་ལ།།
ཉིན་མཚན་བར་མེད་ཞེན་པ་ཉམ་ཐག་གི་འགྲོ་བའི།།
དོན་མེད་བྱ་བཞག་མང་པོ་ཡིད་ཡུལ་དུ་ཤར་ཚེ།།
སྐྱོ་བའི་ཉམས་གླུ་མི་འགུགས་རང་དབང་ནི་མ་བྱུང་།།

The Song Showing Weariness of This Life
The Melodious Cuckoo Singing

1.

The spiritual teacher embodying the wisdom essence of all
buddhas,
the master of the treasure of retention, eloquence, and
excellences,
the lord of buddha families, Mipham, whose wisdom is
immaculate—
please always remain on the lotus in my heart center with joy.

2.

To the dreamlike happiness in this life,
miserable sentient beings cling day and night.
When meaningless trivia appear in my mind,
I could not help singing this song of weariness.

༣

ཕྱུག་པོའི་རྒྱུ་ཞེས་ཀུན་གྱིས་སྨོན་གནས་སུ་བྱེད་མོད།།
ལུས་སེམས་སྡོད་ཁོམ་མེད་པའི་སྡུག་སྡོན་ཞིག་མ་གཏོགས།།
ཟས་གོས་བཟང་པོ་ཙམ་ཡང་ལོངས་སྤྱོད་ནི་མི་བྲ།།
འཆི་ཁ་ཞེན་ཆགས་སྐྱེད་པས་ཐར་ལམ་གྱི་བར་ཆད།།

༤

ཇི་ལྟར་འབྱོར་ཡང་ཟས་གོས་གཉིས་པོ་ཙམ་མ་གཏོགས།།
རང་གི་ཉམས་ལ་ཕན་པ་རྡུལ་ཆ་ཙམ་མེད་ངེས།།
འཛམ་གླིང་རྒྱུ་ནོར་ཡོད་ཚད་མི་གཅིག་ལ་དབང་ཡང་།།
ད་དུང་ཆོག་ཤེས་མི་སྐྱེ་རེ་འདོད་ཀྱིས་གཡེང་འདུག།

༥

ཉམ་ཐག་དབུལ་པོའི་ལུས་ཞེས་ཐམས་ཅད་ཀྱིས་སྨོད་ཀྱང་།།
ཚེ་གང་བར་མེད་གསོག་སྲུང་བརྟག་པ་ཡི་སྡུག་བསྔལ།།
ནོར་མང་ཅན་ལ་འབྱུང་བའི་ངང་ཚུལ་འདི་བསམ་ཚེ།།
སྐྱིད་ཉལ་རང་ལ་དབང་ཕྱིར་སྤྲང་པོ་ཚོ་སྐྱིད་སྙམ།།

3.

So-called wealth has been admired by every being,
but it merely increases the suffering of lacking leisure, physically and mentally.
People splurge on enjoying fine food and clothes,
which only become what they attach to and obstacles to liberation at the time of death.

4.

Even if one becomes wealthy, except for food and clothes,
one will certainly get no other benefit.
Even possessing the wealth of the entire Jambudvipa,
one would not be satisfied but want more.

5.

Although people always mock the destitute,
when I think of what the rich have to experience throughout their lives,
the suffering of seeking, accumulating, and losing wealth,
I prefer to be a happy beggar who has sound sleep and ease.

༤

དབྱར་ཁའི་མེ་ཏོག་འདི་དང་ཕྱུག་པོ་ཡི་རྒྱུ་ནོར།།
ད་ལྟ་མཛེས་མཛེས་འདྲ་ཡང་ནམ་ཕུགས་ནི་ཐུབ་དཀའ།།
སྙིང་པོ་མེད་ལ་ཧ་ཅང་ཞེན་པ་རང་ཆེ་ན།།
བཟོད་དཀའ་ངན་འགྲོའི་གཡང་ལ་འགྲིམ་དགོས་ཞིག་མིན་ནམ།།

༥

གནའ་ཞིག་གླིང་བཞིའི་བདེ་འབྱོར་ཡོད་ཚད་ལ་དབང་བའི།།
ལང་ཚོའི་གོས་རྒྱན་ལྷ་ལ་འགྲན་ནུས་ཀྱི་དཔོན་ཡང་།།
མི་རྟག་མཁའ་ལ་འཇའ་ཚོན་སྣང་བ་བཞིན་ཡལ་ན།།
རང་རེའི་ལོངས་སྤྱོད་རྫ་རྔེའི་ཐིལ་བ་དང་ལོས་འདྲ།།

6.

Summer flowers and the wealth of rich people
both appear gorgeous but cannot last long.
They have no essence, yet kindle excessive attachment,
which tosses us into the unbearable abyss of the lower
realms.

7.

Ancient people used to enjoy the pleasures and wealth of
the entire four continents,
their magnificent clothes and ornaments comparable to
those of the celestial lords,
but these are all as impermanent as rainbows vanishing in
the sky.
Therefore understand that our enjoyment is surely like
dewdrops on a blade of grass.

༨

ན་ནིང་སྣུ་དང་འདྲ་བའི་ཕྲུག་པོ་ནི་ཕལ་ཆེར།།
ད་ལོ་ཉམ་ཐག་སྤྲང་པོའི་གྲལ་མཐའ་ན་འདུག་པ།།
འདི་ཀོ་རྨི་ལམ་མིན་ཡང་རྨི་ལམ་བཞིན་སྣང་ཕྱིར།།
འཁོར་བའི་བདེ་ལ་སྲུན་པ་དབང་མེད་དུ་སྐྱེས་བྱུང་།།

༩

མཐོན་པོའི་ཐོབ་ཅེས་ཀུན་ལ་གྲགས་ཆེན་ཞིག་ཡོད་ད།།
རྟག་བརྟན་མི་འདུག་སྟོན་ཁའི་སྤྲིན་དཀར་གྱི་སྤུན་ཟླ།།
སྙིང་པོ་མེད་པ་དབྱར་གྱི་འཇའ་ཚོན་དངོས་ལགས་ཕྱིར།།
བསམ་ཞིང་བསམས་ན་ཡིད་སྐྱོའི་སྐྱོན་མ་རང་མིན་ནམ།།

༡༠

ཐར་བའི་ལམ་སྟོན་བླ་སེར་མང་པོ་ཡི་ཐུགས་དཀྲུགས།།
ཉེས་མེད་སྡེ་འབངས་ཁྲིམས་ཀྱི་ལས་སྣང་ལ་སྦྱར་ཏེ།།
རང་བཟང་ལྷམ་པའི་ངང་ལ་དུག་སྦྲུལ་བཞིན་འཁྱིལ་ཡང་།།
ཕྱི་མའི་ལམ་འཕྲང་འགྲིམ་དུས་ཅི་འདྲ་ཞིག་ཡོད་གྲང་།།

8.

Most people who were as rich as the king of nagas last year
become the poorest among those bereft of everything this
year.
Since this is not a dream but appears vividly like a dream,
sadness wells up in me and I can't help feeling weary of the
happiness in samsara.

9.

Those in high positions of power are greatly renowned;
this is as impermanent and unsteady as autumn clouds,
and surely has no essence either, like summer rainbows.
When this is pondered over, isn't weariness even stronger?

10.

Disturbing the minds of gurus and the Sangha,
enforcing laws that punish innocent citizens,
acting as arrogant as a poisonous snake—
What can you do when entering subsequent dangerous
passages?

༡༡

ད་ལྟ་རང་སྡེའི་དབུས་ན་མཐོ་མཐོ་ལྟར་སྣང་ཡང་།།
གཤིན་རྗེའི་ཕོ་ཉ་མཐོང་དུས་དེ་ཙམ་ཞིག་མིན་འདྲ།།
ཐར་དཀའ་ངན་སོང་གནས་སུ་སྡུག་བསྔལ་རང་མྱོང་དུས།།
ཡུལ་སྡེ་ལོངས་སྤྱོད་མང་ཡང་ཕན་པ་ནི་མི་གདའ།།

༡༢

མི་རྟག་བཙུད་ལ་རོལ་བའི་བྱུང་བ་ནི་གཞོན་ནུ།།
ཉམས་དགའི་ཚལ་དང་འབྲལ་འདོད་ཡིད་ཡུལ་ན་མེད་ཀྱང་།།
སྟོན་མཇུག་གྲང་ལྷགས་བང་ཆེན་སྔོ་བུར་དུ་ཐོན་དུས།།
སྐྱོ་ཤས་ཡིད་ལ་འཁོར་ཡང་བྱ་ཐབས་དང་བྲལ་འདུག།

༡༣

དེ་བཞིན་ཚེ་འདིར་ཞེན་པའི་སྐྱེ་བོ་ཡི་ཚོགས་ཀྱང་།།
འཆི་བདག་ཕོ་ཉའི་སྡང་མིག་མངོན་སུམ་དུ་མཐོང་ཚེ།།
ཚེ་གཅིག་བག་མེད་སྤྱོད་པས་གཡེང་ཚུལ་ལ་བསམ་དུས།།
འགྱོད་ཆེན་སྙིང་ལ་མཆེད་ཀྱང་འཕྱི་བ་རང་མིན་ནམ།།

11.

Today you have a commanding appearance among people,
but when facing the messenger of the Lord of Death, you
will look different.
When you suffer in the lower realms that are hard to escape,
your immense territory and wealth will be of no use.

12.

The little bee that enjoys flower sap
would not like to leave the beautiful garden,
but when the icy wind suddenly sweeps in at the end of
autumn,
it has no choice but to let weariness linger in its heart.

13.

Human beings desperately clinging to this life—
When you see the wild-eyed messengers of the Lord of
Death,
and recall how carelessly and distractedly you've spent this
life,
isn't it too late for you to bitterly repent at that final
moment?

༡༤

རང་དང་ལྡན་ཅིག་སྐྱེས་ཤིང་ཚེ་གཅིག་ཏུ་གསོས་པའི། །
རང་ལུས་འདི་ཡང་འཁྱེར་བའི་རང་དབང་ཞིག་མེད་ན། །
ཉེ་འབྲེལ་ལོངས་སྤྱོད་ནམ་མཁའི་སྐར་ཚོགས་བཞིན་བཀྲ་ཡང་། །
ཐམས་ཅད་ཤུལ་དུ་བསྐྱུར་ནས་འགྲོ་ངེས་ཤིག་ལོས་ཡིན། །

༡༥

མཐོ་བརྗིད་ཚོན་གྱིས་བྱུགས་པའི་ཁང་བཟང་ནི་མང་པོ། །
མི་བརྟན་གྱང་རལ་བྱེ་མའི་ཕུང་པོ་རུ་འདུག་པའི། །
སྣང་ཚུལ་འདི་ལ་བརྟག་དཔྱད་ཞིབ་མོ་ཞིག་གིས་དང་། །
ཉམས་དགའི་གནས་ལ་ཆགས་ཞེན་ལྷོད་པོ་རུ་གྱུར་ཡོང་། །

༡༦

རང་རེའི་ཕ་དང་མེས་པོ་ཡང་མེས་ཀྱི་རིང་ལ། །
བར་མེད་ཚེ་འདི་གཉེར་ཡང་གྲུབ་ཐབས་ཤིག་མ་བྱུང་། །
བདག་ཀྱང་ཇི་ལྟར་འབད་ཀྱང་དེ་འདྲ་ལས་མེད་ཕྱིར། །
ཟབ་མོའི་ལྷ་ཆོས་བསྒྲུབ་ན་དགའ་ཚོད་ཙམ་མིན་ནམ། །

14.

Being born with me and being fed my entire life,
even my body cannot be taken away with me.
Therefore relatives and possessions, as many as there are
bright stars in the sky,
will certainly be left behind as well when I leave by myself.

15.

The exalted, magnificent, and well-adorned houses
are unstable and will finally fall apart, leaving only remains.
If we carefully ponder this phenomenon,
our desire for pleasant objects will easily quench.

16.

People of my father's and forefathers' generations
have continuously striven their entire lives, but all failed.
Had I exerted myself like them, I would also have no success.
Therefore isn't it joyful to use this life to practice the profound sublime Dharma?

༡༧

ཚེ་སྟོད་དགྲ་སྡེ་མང་པོ་ཚེ་སྨད་ཀྱི་གྲོགས་རེད།།
དེ་རིང་གཅེས་པའི་གྲོགས་ཀྱང་སང་ཉིན་གྱི་དུས་སུ།།
སྲོག་གཅོད་གཤེད་དུ་གྱུར་པའང་སྲིད་པ་ཞིག་ཡིན་ན།།
དགྲ་གཉེན་ངེས་པ་མེད་ལ་ཆགས་སྡང་གིས་ཅི་བྱ།།

༡༨

རང་གི་ལུས་ཀྱིས་བསྐྱེད་པའི་བུ་ཕྲུག་གི་ཚོགས་རྣམས།།
སྙིང་གི་དུམ་བུ་བཞིན་དུ་གཅེས་ཀྲུ་ཡིས་བསྐྱངས་ཀྱང་།།
ནམ་ཞིག་ལུས་སྟོབས་རྫོགས་ནས་དྲིན་ལན་ལ་རེ་དུས།།
ཕན་མེད་ཡི་ཆད་སྐྱེ་བའི་སྨོན་མ་ཞིག་མིན་ནམ།།

༡༩

ལང་ཚོའི་ན་ཚོད་མཉམ་པའི་ན་ཆུང་ཚོ་ཕན་ཚུན།།
འཛུམ་པའི་ཟུར་མིག་གཡོ་བའི་གར་སྟབས་ལ་འཁྲིང་བཞིན།།
ཡིད་མཐུན་ངང་ལ་ཡུན་རིང་འགྲོགས་པ་ལ་སྨོན་ཡང་།།
སྐྱིད་སྡུག་ཅི་འོང་མི་ཤེས་སྙིང་རྗེ་ཞིག་སྐྱེས་བྱུང་།།

17.
Foes of one's early years become friends later on;
one's confidante of today turns into one's killer of tomorrow.
Therefore, since friends and enemies are so uncertain,
what is the use of loving or hating them so much?

18.
Of all your natural offspring
you have taken good care, like parts of your heart.
Yet when they are strong enough to repay your kindness
they do no benefit to you at all; isn't it just more
disappointment?

19.
Young people of the same age
look at each other longingly with smiles.
Although they wish to become intimate companions living
together forever,
since it is unknown whether their future will be joyful or
painful, compassion arises in me.

༢༠

ཡུན་རིང་འགྲོགས་ངེས་མེད་པའི་ཁྱིམ་གཅིག་གི་བཟའ་ཚང་།།
ཚོང་འདུས་མགྲོན་པོ་བཞིན་དུ་ཡུད་ཙམ་ལ་འཚོགས་ཀྱང་།།
སྔོན་བསགས་ལས་ཀྱིས་རིགས་དྲུག་ངེས་མེད་དུ་ཁྲིད་དུས།།
ཕན་ཚུན་གར་སོང་འདིར་ཡོད་སྐྱོགས་ཙམ་ཡང་མི་ཤེས།།

༢༡

བླ་མ་མཆོག་དང་མི་འབྲལ་འགྲོགས་འདོད་ཅིག་ཡོད་མོད།།
སྔོན་བསགས་ལས་ཀྱི་བཀོད་པ་སུ་ཞིག་གིས་ཟློག་ཐུས།།
ཁུ་བྱུག་མོན་ལ་འགྲོ་ཁའི་འདུ་བ་དང་མཚུངས་པའི།།
ཇོ་རྗེའི་མཆེད་ཚོགས་འདི་ཡང་འབྲལ་ངེས་ཤིག་མིན་ནམ།།

༢༢

གོང་གི་རྗེ་དཔོན་བཀུར་ཀྱང་མཉེས་ཐབས་ནི་མི་འདུག།
འོག་གི་ཡུལ་སྤྱི་བསྐྱངས་ཀྱང་མགུ་དུས་ནི་དཀའ་མོ།།
འཁོར་བའི་བྱ་བཞག་འདི་ལ་གྲུབ་དུས་ཤིག་མེད་ཕྱིར།།
བག་ཡངས་བློ་བདེའི་ངང་དུ་ཉལ་ཚོད་ཅིག་མིན་ནམ།།

20.

Family members may or may not live together for a long
time.
They gather together briefly like visitors at a marketplace;
afterward, they head to different destinations of the six
realms based on their past karma,
not knowing each other's whereabouts.

21.

Though unwilling to be separated from the supreme guru,
when it is arranged by previous karma, who is able to avert it?
Just as when the time comes for cuckoos to fly south,
Vajra brothers and sisters have to separate.

22.

No matter how you pay reverence to a superior lord,
you cannot make him happy;
no matter how much you protect inferior subordinates,
they are not satisfied.
Since there is no end of samsaric trivia,
isn't it nice to relax and have a relieved and peaceful mind?

༢༣

དགྲ་བོ་ཇི་ལྟར་བཏུལ་ཀྱང་ཇེ་མང་ལས་མི་གདའ། །
ཉེ་འབྲེལ་བྱམས་པས་བསྐྱངས་ཀྱང་དགའ་སྡུག་ནི་ཇེ་མང་། །
བཟང་རྒྱུའི་ཟས་མང་ཟོས་ཀྱང་མི་གཙང་གི་སྣོན་མ། །
ད་ནི་མདོ་མེད་སྤྲང་པོའི་སྤྱོད་ཚུལ་ལ་དགྱེས་རན། །

༢༤

ཕར་ལ་སྙིང་བཞིན་བསྐྱངས་པའི་ཡིད་མཐུན་གྱི་གྲོགས་ཀྱང་། །
ཚུར་ལ་མངོན་ལྐོག་མེད་པར་དགའ་ཚོད་ཅིག་མིན་པར། །
ཁོ་རང་བློ་ཅེ་ན་ཆུང་གསར་བ་ལ་གཏོད་འདུག །
གྲོགས་མེད་གཅིག་པུར་བསྡད་ན་སྐྱིད་པོ་ཞིག་མིན་ནམ། །

༢༥

མཁས་བཙུན་བཟང་གསུམ་འཛོམས་པའི་བཤེས་གཉེན་གྱི་ཚོགས་
ཀྱང་། །
དང་པོར་མཇལ་དུས་ཐམས་ཅད་བརྩེ་བཀུར་ལ་སྤྲོ་ཡང་། །
རྒྱུན་དུ་འགྲོགས་ན་ངན་བརྗོད་ཁོ་ན་ལ་བརྩོན་ཕྱིར། །
སྙིགས་མའི་འགྲོ་དོན་རང་རེས་འགྲུབ་ཐབས་ནི་དཀའ་བ། །

23.

To overcome enemies only makes them multiply,
to kindly protect relatives only creates more afflictions,
to consume fine food only generates more filth—
therefore I would take a beggar's way of life from now on.

24.

Friends that you care so much about, like your own heart,
return no genuine affection openly or secretly,
but pour all their affection on their new friends—
therefore isn't it happy to be alone with no companion?

25.

When coming across learned, righteous, and excellent
spiritual teachers,
people cheerfully pay respect at the beginning,
but after being around for a while they say only bad words—
therefore it is hard for us to benefit sentient beings of the
degeneration time.

༢༦

ཡོན་ཏན་ཅན་གྱི་སྐྱེ་བོར་བསྟོད་བསྔགས་ནི་མི་བརྗོད།།
ངན་སྤྱོད་ཕྲན་བུ་ཐོས་ཚེ་བརྟག་དཔྱད་ཙམ་མེད་པར།།
མཐོང་ཚད་མི་ལ་ཁྲབ་བརྫལ་སྨྲེལ་བ་ལ་བརྩོན་པའི།།
སྐྱེ་རྒྱུའི་རང་གཤིས་འདི་ལ་ཅིའི་ཕྱིར་ན་མི་སྐྱོ།།

༢༧

རང་ཡུལ་བཞུགས་པའི་མཁས་གྲུབ་མིག་ལམ་ནས་བོར་ཏེ།།
གཞན་ནས་འོངས་པའི་མགོ་བསྐོར་ཐབས་ཚུལ་ལ་མཁས་པའི།།
རྫུན་ཅན་སྐྱེ་བོ་ལྷ་བཞིན་བཀུར་ཚུལ་ལ་བསམ་ཚེ།།
རྒྱལ་བསྟན་ཉུབ་ལ་ཉེ་བའི་རང་རྟགས་དངོས་ཡིན་སྙམ།།

༢༨

བསྟན་འཛིན་རྒྱན་མཆོག་ཚུལ་ཁྲིམས་ཤེས་རབ་གཉིས་ཡིན་ཡང་།།
དེང་སང་ཡོན་ཏན་ཅན་ལ་བསྟི་བཀུར་ནི་མི་བྱེད།།
དར་གོས་རྒྱན་གྱིས་མཛེས་པའི་སྤྲུལ་མིང་ཙམ་ཐོགས་རྣམས།།
ཡོན་ཏན་སྣ་གཅིག་མེད་ཀྱང་ངོ་སོ་རང་མཐོ་འདུག།

26.

Many people never praise others' excellent qualities,
yet when hearing about others' minute misdeeds
they spread it to whomever they come across without first
making the slightest examination.
How can I not be weary of such characters?

27.

Many people look down on their local learned masters,
yet when outside deceivers good at cheating come
they reverently pay homage to those untruthful charlatans.
Isn't it a sign of the ending of Buddhism?

28.

Discipline and wisdom are the two ornaments to uphold the
teachings,
but people nowadays do not honor these qualities.
Thereby those silk- and brocade-adorned so-called tulkus,
though they have no good qualities, are highly respected.

༢༩

ངན་སྐྱོན་འབུམ་གྱིས་གང་བའི་ངང་ཚུལ་ལ་མི་དཔྱད།།
མངོན་ཕྱོག་ཀུན་ཏུ་གཞན་སྐྱོན་བརྗོད་པ་ལ་བརྩོན་པའི།།
རང་དང་ཤིན་ཏུ་མཚུངས་པའི་གྲོགས་པོ་ཚོ་མཐོང་ཚེ།།
ཡིད་སྐྱོའི་སེམས་འདི་སྙིང་གི་ཐིག་ལེ་ལ་འཁོར་འདུག།

༣༠

བསགས་པའི་འབྲུ་དྲུག་སྔོན་མོ་ཞིང་ནང་དུ་བཏབ་སྟེ།།
སྟོན་དུས་འབྲས་བུ་སྨིན་དུས་སྐྱོད་སྙམ་ཞིག་ཡོད་ཀྱང་།།
སྙོན་མེད་རིམ་གྱིས་ཕྲི་བ་མི་ཚེ་ཡི་སྣང་བ།།
དེ་ཡི་སྟོན་ལ་མི་འཛད་དཔའ་གདེང་ནི་ཅི་ཡོད།།

༣༡

ངེས་པར་འཆི་སྙམ་ཙམ་ཞིག་བློ་ཡུལ་ན་ཡོད་ཀྱང་།།
ནམ་འཆི་ཆ་མེད་སྒོམ་པའི་བརྩོན་འགྲུས་ནི་མ་བྱས།།
སྐྱེས་ནས་ད་ལྟའི་བར་ལ་ལོ་མང་ཞིག་སོང་ཡང་།།
ལྷ་ཆོས་འདི་འགྲུབ་སྙམ་པའི་དཔའ་གདེང་ནི་མི་གདའ།།

29.

Many people never examine their disposition to overflown
faults,
but diligently spread others' mistakes overtly and secretly.
When seeing such friends as I do myself,
sadness wells up and lingers in my heart center.

30.

Although you wish to sow six kinds of grains in the field,
and enjoy the mature harvest in the fall,
since our lifespan keeps decreasing, with no increase,
who can be sure that death will not come before?

31.

Although I strongly believe death is certain,
since I have not diligently practiced on the uncertainty of the
time of death,
and from birth until now have already lived so many years,
I have no confidence that I can accomplish this noble
Dharma.

༣༢

ངམ་ངམ་ཤུགས་ལ་འགྲུབ་པ་སྡིག་ལྟུང་གི་རྣམ་གྲངས།།
མང་མང་བསགས་པའི་སྤྱོད་པ་བློ་ཡུལ་དུ་མི་ཤོང་།།
དེ་རིང་ཙམ་ལ་འཆི་བདག་ལས་མཁན་པོ་ཐོན་ན།།
འགྲོ་ས་ངན་སོང་གནས་ལས་གཞན་ཞིག་ནི་མེད་འདྲ།།

༣༣

དལ་འབྱོར་ཐོབ་ཀྱང་ཆོས་ཀྱི་སྙིང་པོ་ནི་མ་ལོན།།
བླ་མ་མཛལ་ཡང་དགོངས་སྤྱོད་སློབ་པ་ལ་མ་བརྩོན།།
གདམས་ཟབ་ཐོབ་རུང་ཉོན་མོངས་གཉེན་པོ་རུ་མ་སོང་།།
ཚེ་གང་དོན་མེད་གྱུར་ལ་འགྱོད་ཆེན་ཞིག་སྐྱེས་བྱུང་།།

32.

If the misdeeds and downfalls that I have committed
are counted, the number could not be held in my mind.
If the Lord of Death suddenly arrives today,
the only place that I could go would be the lower realms.

33.

Although I have obtained the endowment and leisure,
I have not tasted the essence of the Dharma.
Although I have met the Supreme Guru, I have not
diligently emulated his realization and actions.
Although I have received the profound instructions,
I have not pacified afflictions.
Since I have lived an entire life futilely, great repentance
arises in me.

༣༤

ད་ནི་ཚེ་མཇུག་འདི་ལ་དགེ་ཆོས་རང་བསྒྲུབས་ནས། །
སྔར་བྱས་སྡིག་ལྟུང་རྣམ་སྨིན་ལྷག་མེད་དུ་བྱང་སྟེ། །
འཆི་ཁ་འཁྲུགས་པ་མེད་པའི་དམ་ཆོས་ཤིག་འགྲུབ་པའི། །
བྱིན་རླབས་ཆར་དུ་སྤེལ་ཤོག་དྲིན་ཆེན་གྱི་བླ་མ། །

༣༥

དག་དང་མ་དག་ཞིང་ཁམས་རབ་འབྱམས་ཀྱི་ཁྱོན་དུ། །
མི་དང་མི་མིན་བྱ་སོགས་མ་ངེས་པའི་གཟུགས་ཀྱིས། །
འཇམ་མགོན་བླ་མས་འགྲོ་དོན་མཛད་པ་ཡི་དྲུང་དུ། །
བདག་ཀྱང་འབྲལ་མེད་འཁོད་པའི་དགེ་ལེགས་ལ་སློན་ནོ། །

༣༦

རིང་ནས་དྲིན་གྱིས་བསྐྱངས་པ་མ་གྱུར་གྱི་སེམས་ཅན། །
གཅིག་ཀྱང་མི་ལྷག་བདེ་ཆེན་དག་པ་ཡི་ཞིང་དུ། །
བདེ་བླག་འཁྲིད་པའི་སྟོབས་ཤུགས་བདག་གཅིག་ལ་དབང་ནས། །
འཇམ་མགོན་བླ་མའི་བཞེད་དོན་འགྲུབ་ནུས་སུ་གྱུར་ཅིག །

34.

From now on, for the rest of my life I will practice virtue,
confessing and purifying my past misdeeds and downfalls
without remainder.
I supplicate my kind guru to bestow the rain of blessing—
the accomplishment of no regret at the time of death.

35.

In all the pure and impure realms,
and with human and nonhuman forms,
while my Manjushri guru benefits sentient beings,
may I always be in front of him without separation.

36.

May all mother sentient beings who have nurtured me with
kindness since beginningless time,
be easily directed to Dewachen without exception,
and I myself alone will master such strength,
to fulfill the wishes of my Manjushri guru.

༣༧

སྒྲ་འདི་སུ་ཡི་རྣ་བར་སོན་པ་དང་མཉམ་དུ།།
འདི་སྣང་ཞེན་པའི་ཀུན་རྟོག་ན་བུན་བཞིན་སངས་ཏེ།།
མ་འབད་བཞིན་དུ་བྱང་ཕྱོགས་སོ་བདུན་ལ་དབང་ནས།།
དོན་གཉིས་མཐར་སོན་སྟོབས་བཅུའི་བདག་པོ་རུ་གྱུར་ཅིག།

ཅེས་ཚོགས་སུ་བཅད་པ་བྱང་ཕྱོགས་སོ་བདུན་གྱི་གྲངས་ལྡན་འདི་ནི་རབ་རྒྱལ་ཤིང་འབྲུག་ཟླ་༧ཚེས་༢༠ལ་ངག་དབང་བློ་གྲོས་མཚུངས་མེད་པའི་ཁ་ནས་གང་བྱུང་བསྒྱུར་བཅོས་སྤུ་ཙམ་མ་བྱས་པར་ཡུད་ཙམ་ཞིག་ལ་སྤེལ་བ་མངྒ་ལཾ།། །།

37.

Whoever hears this song,
may their attachment to this life vanish as mist disperses,
may they effortlessly master the thirty-seven factors of enlightenment,
perfect the two benefits, and become the lord of the ten powers.

This poem with verses of the same number as the thirty-seven factors of enlightenment (*rgyal sras lag len so bdun ma*), was immediately written down without the slightest modification after Ngawang Lodrö Tsungmed (Jigme Phuntsok Rinpoche) uttered them without thinking. Mangalam! (May all be auspicious!)

༄༅། །གསོལ་འདེབས་བྱིན་རླབས་ཉི་འོད།

༄༅། །དུས་གསུམ་རྒྱལ་བ་ཐམས་ཅད་འདུས་པའི་སྐུ། །
མ་ལུས་འགྲོ་ཀུན་འདྲེན་པའི་དེད་དཔོན་མཆོག །
མཁའ་འགྲོ་རྒྱ་མཚོའི་ཚོགས་དཔོན་ཧེ་རུ་ཀ །
ཡིད་བཞིན་ནོར་བུ་ཁྱེད་ལ་སྙིང་ནས་འདུད། །

ཁྱོད་ལས་ལྷག་པའི་བླ་མ་བདག་ལ་མེད། །
ཁྱོད་ཀྱི་གསུང་ལས་ཉམས་ལེན་གཞན་དུ་མེད། །
དུས་ཀུན་རེ་ལྟོས་གཅིག་པུར་ཁྱོད་བསྟེན་ན། །
ཡིད་བཞིན་ནོར་ཞེས་འབོད་པ་དོན་ལྡན་མཛོད། །

Pray to the Guru
The Sunlight of Blessings

The embodiment of all the buddhas of the three times,
the supreme captain guiding all sentient beings,
the chief deity of all sky dancers, Heruka—
to you, Guru Wish-Fulfilling Jewel, I pay homage.

My supreme guru!
When meditating, I follow only your instructions.
My sole protector!
I persistently rely on you, the veritable Wish-Fulfilling Jewel!

བདག་ནི་བློ་དམན་སྦྱངས་པ་ཆུང་བས་ན།།
སྦྱོང་ཀློག་རྒྱ་ཆེར་བྱེད་ལ་མཐུ་ཆུང་ཡང་།།
བླ་མ་མཆོག་དང་འཇམ་དཔལ་གཞོན་ནུ་ཟུང་།།
དབྱེར་མེད་སྤྱི་བོའི་གཙུག་གམ་སྙིང་དབུས་སུ།།

བཞུགས་པར་མོས་ནས་གསོལ་བ་འདེབས་ལགས་ན།།
བྱིན་རླབས་ཐུགས་རྗེའི་བགོ་སྐལ་མི་དམན་པར།།
དབང་གིས་སྨིན་ཅིང་གདམས་པས་རྒྱུད་གྲོལ་ཏེ།།
སྣང་བཞི་མཐར་ཏུ་འཁྱོལ་བར་བྱིན་གྱིས་རློབས།།

My wisdom is inferior, my meditation is rudimentary,
my capacity for extensive study is low.
So, my supreme guru, inseparable from the ever-youthful
Manjushri,
please always reside on the crown of my head or in the center
of my heart.

With devotion, I sincerely pray to you.
Please kindly bestow favorable conditions,
ripen me through empowerment, liberate me with
instructions.
And may the four visions of my practice reach
consummation!

སྐྱེ་བ་ཀུན་ཏུ་ཁྱེད་དང་མི་འབྲལ་ཞིང་།།
ཏིང་འཛིན་ཡོན་ཏན་རྒྱ་མཚོའི་གཉེར་ལ་དབང་།།
འཇམ་དཔལ་དབྱངས་བཞིན་ནམ་མཁའ་ཇི་སྲིད་དུ།།
མ་ལུས་འགྲོ་བའི་དོན་ལ་བརྩོན་གྱུར་ཅིག།

ཅེས་སློབ་བུ་དམ་པ་རིག་དོན་གྱི་ངོར་རི་བོ་རྩེ་ལྔའི་ཡང་དབེན་དུ་ངག་དབང་བློ་གྲོས་མཚུངས་མེད་པས་བྲིས་པ་དགེ། །།

May I never be separated from you in this and every future life;
by mastering the ocean-like treasure of meditative absorption and excellent qualities,
may I, like Manjushri, diligently work for the benefit of all sentient beings
until the end of space.

This prayer was composed by Ngawang Lodrö Tsungmed (Jigme Phuntsok Rinpoche) at the request of the virtuous disciple Rigdon in the solitary place, Mount Wutai. Excellent!

༄། །རྣལ་འབྱོར་སྙིད་པའི་ཉམས་གླུ་བཀྲ་ཤིས་དོན་ཀུན་གྲུབ་པའི་སྒྲ་དབྱངས་ཞེས་བྱ་བ་བཞུགས།།

༄། །ཚེ་རབས་ལས་ཀྱི་ཕྲེང་བར་སྤྱི་གཙུག་གི་རྒྱན་དུ།།
འབྲལ་མེད་ལས་སྨོན་དཀར་པོས་མི་ཧྲོག་གིས་བཅིང་བའི།།
མཚུངས་མེད་དྲིན་ཆེན་བླ་མ་ཡིད་བཞིན་གྱི་ནོར་བུ།།
མཚན་གྱིས་བརྗོད་དཀའ་ཐུབ་བསྟན་ཆོས་འཕེལ་དེ་མཁྱེན་ནོ།།

སྙིང་དབུས་མི་ཤིགས་འཁོར་ལོའི་གུར་ཁང་གི་དབུས་སུ།།
འབྲལ་མེད་དད་གསུམ་བདུད་རྩིས་མཆོད་སྤྲིན་གྱིས་བསྟེན་པའི།།
རིགས་བརྒྱའི་ཁྱབ་བདག་མི་ཕམ་བློ་གྲོས་ནི་དྲི་མེད།།
གཟུངས་སྤོབས་ཡོན་ཏན་བྱེ་བའི་གཏེར་མཛོད་ཁྱེད་མཁྱེན་ནོ།།

Happy Song of the Yogi

The Auspicious and Wish-Fulfilling Melody

In all lifetimes, you are the never-parting crown ornament
adorned with pure flowers of karmic connection and
aspirations—
my peerless kind guru, Wish-Fulfilling Jewel,
Thupten Chöphel, the name I hesitate to utter.
Please take me in your care!

Always in the palace of the heart center of the inexhaustible
mind wheel,
with the ambrosia-offering clouds of the three faiths,
is the master of the one hundred families—Mipham
Rinpoche, immaculate wisdom,
the treasure of infinite qualities of dharani and debating
skills.
Please take me in your care!

དེ་རང་དགའ་འོ་སྐྱིད་དོ་བླ་མ་ཡི་ཐུགས་རྗེས།།
བསམ་དོན་དམ་ཆོས་འདུན་མ་ཡིད་བཞིན་དུ་འགྲུབ་ནས།།
རྒས་པའི་ལུས་འདི་གར་ལ་འཁྱོལ་ཐབས་ཤིགས་མེད་ཀྱང་།།
སྐྱིད་པའི་སྨྱུ་ཆུང་མལ་ནས་ཐོལ་བྱུང་དུ་འགུགས་འདོད།།

རིགས་དྲུག་འཁོར་བའི་གནས་ན་སྐྱིད་སྡུག་གི་ལས་སྣང་།།
དཀར་ནག་སོས་ཀའི་སྤྲིན་བཞིན་རྟག་བརྟན་ཞིག་མེད་ཀྱང་།།
ང་ཅག་དམ་ཆོས་སྤྱོད་པའི་སྐལ་བཟང་གི་སྐྱེ་བོ།།
བདེ་ནས་བདེ་བར་འགྲོ་ཕྱིར་སྐྱིད་པོ་ཅུ་འདུག་གོ།

From the compassion of the guru I have attained present
happiness and bliss,
and my wish to practice the genuine Dharma has also been
fulfilled.
Although my decrepit body cannot dance joyfully any more,
I could not help singing this impromptu happy song in bed.

Happiness and suffering, the karmic results in the six realms
of samsara,
alternate as black and white, wavering like the ever-changing
clouds in autumn.
What sublime happiness for us practitioners with great
fortune
to travel from happiness to happiness!

ལས་སྨོན་ཁུ་བྱུག་བུ་མོས་སྒྲ་དབྱངས་ཀྱིས་བསྐུལ་ནས།།
ཆུང་ནས་ཐུབ་བསྟན་ནགས་མའི་སྐྱིད་ཚལ་ལ་ཕེབས་ཏེ།།
ཐེག་མཆོག་བདུད་རྩིའི་ཟེགས་མའི་བཅུད་ལེན་ལ་རོལ་བས།།
ཐོགས་མའི་རྟེན་འབྲེལ་དམ་པའི་ཆོས་ཕྱོགས་ལ་འགྲིགས་སོང་།།

སྔོན་བྱོན་དམ་པའི་རྣམ་ཐར་ཡིད་ཡུལ་ལ་བཅིང་སྟེ།།
མཚུངས་མེད་བླ་མ་དམ་པའི་ཞལ་གསུང་ལ་ཉན་ནས།།
སྟོན་འཁོར་ཉམས་དགའ་འཛོམས་པ་ད་ལྟ་ཡང་དྲན་ན།།
ལུས་སེམས་སྤོད་མི་ཚུགས་པའི་དགའ་སྤྲོ་ཞིག་འདུག་པ།།

Having been encouraged by the melodious singing of the
cuckoo owing to past aspirations,
I was fortunate to enter the garden of the sublime Dharma
when still very young,
and have enjoyed the ambrosia essence of the Supreme
Vehicle since then.
The initial favorable circumstances for the sublime Dharma
are also present.

The biographies of great masters of the past have been
engraved in my mind;
the instructions of my peerless guru have been listened to
with my very ears.
Today when I look back on the happy gathering of the guru
and disciples,
I am extremely happy and cannot calm myself physically or
mentally.

སྐྱབས་གནས་རྒྱ་མཚོའི་སྤྱི་གཟུགས་བླ་མ་ནི་རྗེ་ཡི།།
ཐུགས་རྗེ་ན་བཟའ་དཀར་པོའི་གྲྭ་མཐའ་ལ་འཇུས་ནས།།
ནམ་ཡང་འབྲལ་བ་མེད་པའི་སྨོན་ལམ་ཞིག་བཏབ་ཡོད།།
ད་ནི་ཇི་ལྟར་བྱས་ཀྱང་སྐྱིད་པོ་རུ་འདུག་གོ།

ཕ་མེས་རིག་འཛིན་བརྒྱུད་པའི་ཐུགས་དམ་གྱི་སྐྱེལ་སོ།།
འཇའ་ལུས་ཆོས་སྐུ་གྲུབ་པའི་ཐེག་རྩེ་ཡི་ཆོས་ཚུལ།།
འདི་དང་འཕྲད་ཚད་སྲིད་པ་ཐ་མ་རུ་ངེས་པས།།
བློ་ཕུགས་ཁོང་ལ་བཅོལ་བའི་རྣལ་འབྱོར་ང་སྐྱིད་པ།།

Once, holding tightly the hem of my peerless kind guru,
the embodiment of the ocean-like entire refuge fields,
I made the virtuous aspiration never to part from him in any
lifetime.
Now, whatever I encounter or do I feel equally happy.

The ultimate essence of Vidyadhara lineage masters of the
past,
the Dharma of the Pinnacle Vehicle leading to accomplish
the rainbow body dharmakāya—
anyone coming across it will surely cease to roam in samsara.
Since it has been entrusted to me, the yogi, I am extremely
happy.

རིགས་ཀུན་ཁྱབ་བདག་མི་ཕམ་སློ་གྲོས་ནི་དྲི་མེད།།
སོས་གྲུས་དད་པའི་ཡིད་མཁར་འབྲལ་མེད་དུ་བསྟེན་པས།།
རིག་སྟོང་གཅུག་མ་རྡོ་རྗེའི་རང་ཚུགས་ཤིག་ཟིན་ཏེ།།
ཡིད་དཔྱོད་བཅོས་མའི་ལྷ་སྒོམ་ཡིད་ཡུལ་ནས་ཐོར་སོང་།།

སྤུག་འབད་ཨུ་ཚུགས་བརྩོན་པའི་དཔེ་ཀློག་ལ་མ་ལྟོས།།
གཟུང་འཛིན་སེམས་ཀྱི་འདུད་རྒྱ་སྙིང་དབུས་ནས་གྲོལ་བས།།
མདོ་སྔགས་གཞུང་བརྒྱའི་གནད་གསང་རྩོལ་མེད་དུ་ཤར་བའི།།
ཐེག་རྩེའི་གསང་ལམ་སྙིགས་པའི་རྣལ་འབྱོར་ང་སྐྱིད་པ།།

The master of all families, Venerable Mipham of immaculate wisdom!
I constantly rely on you with a mind of devotion and reverence.
Having realized the primordial Vajra state of awareness and emptiness,
I dispel all contrived mental fabrications and views, and practice from my heart.

Without any forced diligent listening or reflecting,
the mind bondage of dualism has disengaged from my heart center
and the secret essence of the hundred sutras and tantras has spontaneously appeared.
As a yogi on the secret path of the Pinnacle Vehicle, I am extremely happy!

དམིགས་མེད་བྱམས་དང་སྙིང་རྗེས་ལྷག་བསམ་གྱིས་བསྐུལ་ནས།།
འབྲེལ་ཚད་འགྲོ་ཀུན་དག་པའི་ཞིང་བཟང་དུ་ཁྲིད་ཕྱིར།།
ཞུམ་མེད་སྙིང་སྟོབས་བརྩོན་པའི་གོ་ཆ་ཞིག་བགོས་ནས།།
གཞན་དོན་ཡིད་བཞིན་འགྲུབ་པའི་རྣལ་འབྱོར་ང་སྐྱིད་པ།།

ཕན་བདེའི་འབྱུང་གནས་ཐུབ་བསྟན་རིན་ཆེན་གྱི་ཏོག་བཟང་།།
ཚེར་སྙིགས་ཐུན་གསུམ་འཁོར་ལོའི་སྨག་རུམ་དུ་གནས་པ།།
བཤད་སྒྲུབ་རྒྱལ་མཚན་དཀར་པོའི་རྩེ་མོ་རུ་བཏེགས་ནས།།
བསྟན་པའི་ཞབས་ཏོག་འགྲུབ་པའི་རྣལ་འབྱོར་ང་སྐྱིད་པ།།

Encouraged by the supreme mind of nonreferential kindness
and compassion,
in order to guide sentient beings with fortune to the Pure
Land,[1]
as a yogi who has donned the fearless armor of fortitude and
diligence
to benefit others as I wish, I am extremely happy!

The wonderful jewel of Buddhadharma is the source of
happiness and bliss
in this dark and gloomy deep night of the degeneration time.
As a yogi who places the jewel on the white victory-banner
crown of teaching and practicing
to spread Buddhadharma, I am extremely happy!

འབྱུང་འདུས་སྒྱུ་མའི་ཕུང་པོ་ཟག་བཅས་ཀྱི་འཁྲུལ་འཁོར།།
བར་མེད་ན་དང་རྒ་བའི་དུཿཁ་ཡིས་ཟིན་ཀྱང་།།
དལ་འབྱོར་མི་ཚེ་དོན་ལྡན་དམ་ཆོས་ཀྱིས་འབྱོལ་བས།།
སེམས་ལ་གྲུ་ཡང་སྐྱིད་ཀྱི་ཉི་མ་ཞིག་ཤར་འདུག།

ད་ནི་རྩ་གསུམ་ལྷ་དང་བླ་མ་ཡི་དགྱེས་བརྙེས།།
དབུགས་དབྱུང་གསང་གཏམ་རོལ་མོ་རྫ་བ་རྟ་སྒོན་ནས།།
བདེ་ནས་བདེ་བར་འགྲོ་བའི་གདེང་ཆེན་ཞིག་རྙེད་དེ།།
གཅིག་པུར་གནས་ཀྱང་སྐྱིད་པའི་ཉམས་སྨྱུ་ཞིག་འགུགས་འདོད།།

The contaminated illusory body of the aggregated four great elements
is constantly tortured by the suffering of illness and aging,
but since this human body with leisure and endowment can practice the sublime Buddhadharma life-long,
a resplendent sun of happiness freely arises in my heart!

I have heard the compassionate comforting secret words
from the three roots, the deity, and the guru today.
I have gained the great certainty of traveling from happiness to happiness.
Though being alone, I still could not help singing a Dharma song of happiness!

གསོན་ཀྱང་དགའ་སྐྱེ་བསྟན་འགྲོའི་དོན་ཆེན་ཞིག་འགྲུབ་འདུག །
ཤི་ཡང་དགའ་སྐྱེ་དག་པའི་ཞིང་ཁམས་ལ་འགྲོ་ངེས།།
སྐྱིད་སྡུག་ལས་ཀྱི་སྣང་བ་ཇི་འདྲ་ཞིག་བྱུང་ཡང་།།
ཡིད་ལ་རེ་དང་དོགས་པའི་སེམས་ཁྲལ་དེ་བོར་སོང་།།

ནམ་ཞིག་ཟག་བཅས་ཕུང་པོའི་སྦུབས་ཀྱུ་ལས་གྲོལ་ཚེ།།
དབང་མེད་ལས་ཀྱིས་བསྐྱེད་པའི་སྒྱུ་ལུས་འདིས་སུན་ནས།།
བདེ་ལྡན་དག་པའི་ཞིང་གི་མེ་ཏོག་གི་སྙིང་པོར།།
ཡིད་འོང་མཚན་དཔེས་མཛེས་པའི་ལུས་མཆོག་ཅིག་ལེན་འདོད།།

To be alive, I am joyful because I can spread the Dharma and
benefit sentient beings.
To die, I am happy because I will surely take birth in the
Pure Land.
No matter, coming across whatever karmic phenomena,
whether misery or happiness,
I have given up the worrying mind state of hope and fear!

Once freed from the shell of the contaminated aggregated
body,
I will abandon this karmic illusory body,
take birth in the lotus of the Pure Land of Bliss,
and obtain the pleasant sublime body bearing the major and
minor marks.

སངས་རྒྱས་དངོས་ལས་ཐེག་མཆོག་གདམ་པ་ཞིག་མནོས་ནས། །
རྫོགས་པའི་ལུས་སྟོབས་རྫོགས་ཏེ་སྤྲུལ་བ་ཡི་རོལ་གར། །
རིག་འཛིན་སེམས་དཔའ་སེམས་མའི་མཛའ་གྲོགས་དང་བལྡེབས་
ནས། །
དག་དང་མ་དག་ཞིང་དུ་ལྷུད་མོ་ཏུ་ཕེབས་འགྲོ། །

མདོར་ན་ད་ནས་བརྩོན་པའི་གོ་ཆ་ཞིག་བགོས་ཏེ། །
ཀུན་བཟང་སྤྱོད་པ་རྒྱ་མཚོའི་རྣམ་ཐར་ལ་བསླབས་ནས། །
མ་རྒན་འགྲོ་ཀུན་སྲིད་པའི་རྒྱ་མཚོ་ལས་སྒྲོལ་ཕྱིར། །
ནམ་མཁའ་སྲིད་དུ་བརྩོན་ལ་སྤྲོ་བ་ཞིག་སྐྱེས་བྱུང་། །

I have heard the teachings of the Supreme Vehicle from my guru, a real buddha,
and perfected the enlightened body strength with illusory display.
Accompanied by heroes and heroines of Vidyadharas,
I travel around all the pure and impure realms!

In brief, from now on I will don the armor of diligence
and take the ocean-like actions of Bodhisattva Samantabhadra
in order to free all mother sentient beings from the ocean of samsara.
May I be diligent and joyful until the end of space!

དེ་ལྟར་ཡོངས་སྤྱོད་འཁོར་ལོའི་རོལ་མོ་ཡི་དབྱངས་སྙན།།
བཀྲ་ཤིས་དོན་ཀུན་གྲུབ་པའི་དགའ་སྐྱིད་ཀྱི་དོ་ཧ།།
འདི་ཉིད་རྣ་བར་སོན་པའི་མཆོག་དམན་གྱི་འགྲོ་ཀུན།།
རྟག་ཏུ་སྨྲ་ངན་མེད་པའི་དཔལ་ཡོན་ལ་སྨོན་ནོ།།

ཞེས་པ་འདི་ནི་བོད་རབ་བྱུང་༡༧པའི་ས་ཡོས་ས་ག་ཟླ་བའི་ཚེས་༢ཀྱི་
ཕུ་རྡོའི་ཆར་ངག་དབང་བློ་གྲོས་མཚུངས་མེད་པས་གང་ཤར་བཅོས་
བསྐྱུར་མ་བྱས་པར་སྨྲས་པ་དགེའོ།། །།

When this enjoyment wheel of wonderful sound,
the auspicious wish-fulfilling joyful Dharma song,
is heard by any sentient being, superior or inferior,
may they constantly be free from worry and sadness, yet be glorious.

I, Ngawang Lodrö Tsungmed, wrote down these words that naturally effused from my heart in the morning on the second day of the saga month (the fourth month) of the fire-rabbit year (1987). May all be virtuous!

༄། །ཚེ་རབས་རྗེས་འཛིན་སྨོན་ལམ། །

དུས་གསུམ་གཤེགས་པའི་རྒྱལ་བ་ཐམས་ཅད་ཀུན། །
རང་ངོར་བཞེས་གཉེན་མཆོག་གི་སྐུར་སྣང་བ། །
བཀའ་དྲིན་མཚུངས་བྲལ་ཡོན་ཏན་རྒྱ་མཚོའི་གཏེར། །
ཡིད་བཞིན་ནོར་བུ་ཁྱེད་ལ་གསོལ་བ་འདེབས། །

ཁྱེད་ཀྱིས་འགྲོ་འདུལ་ཐབས་མཁས་སྤྱོད་པ་ནི། །
རྣམ་པ་སྣ་ཚོགས་ཇི་ལྟར་བསྟན་གྱུར་ཀྱང་། །
སྐད་ཅིག་ཙམ་ཡང་ལོག་ལྟ་མི་སྐྱེ་བར། །
ཇི་མཛད་ལེགས་པར་མཐོང་བར་བྱིན་གྱིས་རློབས། །

Prayer for Acceptance by the Guru in All Lifetimes

Embodying all the Gone to Bliss of the three times,
you have appeared as the Supreme Guru before me.
An ocean-like treasury is your unsurpassable kindness and
excellent qualities.
To you, my Wish-Fulfilling Jewel, I pray.

In order to liberate sentient beings, whatever skillful means
and actions you take,
whatever kinds of appearances you manifest,
may I hold no negative attitude even for an instant,
and view all your activities as virtuous.

གང་གིས་བརྩེ་བར་གདམས་པའི་གསུང་བཟང་ལས། །
ཚིག་ཟུར་ཙམ་ཡང་འགོངས་པར་མི་བྱེད་ཅིང༌། །
བུམ་པ་གང་བྱོའི་ཚུལ་གྱིས་བྱིན་རླབས་ཀུན། །
མ་ལུས་བདག་གི་རྒྱུད་ལ་འཕོ་བར་ཤོག །

མགོན་ཁྱོད་དག་དང་མ་དག་ཞིང་རྣམས་སུ། །
སྣ་ཚོགས་སྤྲུལ་པའི་རོལ་གར་རྩོམ་པའི་ཚེ། །
བདག་ཀྱང་ཁྱོད་ཀྱི་ཞབས་འབྲང་མཆོག་གྱུར་ནས། །
བྱང་ཆུབ་སྤྱོད་ལ་མཉམ་དུ་འཇུག་པར་ཤོག །

ནམ་ཞིག་རང་སྣང་དག་པའི་ཞིང་མཆོག་ཏུ། །
རྗེ་ཁྱོད་མངོན་འཚང་རྒྱ་བའི་ཚུལ་སྟོན་ཚེ། །
བདག་ཀྱང་འདུས་པ་དང་པོའི་གྲལ་འཁོད་དེ། །
ཕྲིན་ལས་སྤེལ་བའི་བྱེད་པོ་མཆོག་ཏུ་སྨོན། །

Any piece of compassionate advice from you,
even if it is a word or two, I will never transgress.
Like pouring water into a vase, may all blessings
completely dissolve into my mindstream.

Protector, in all realms, pure and turbid,
when you manifest in various forms of illusory display,
may I in good fortune become your supreme retinue
and engage in the bodhisattva's way of life.

In the supreme pure realm of self-display,
Lord, when you reach full enlightenment,
may I become one of your first disciples
and increase the prosperity of your enlightened activities.

མདོར་ན་ད་ནས་སྐྱེ་བ་ཐམས་ཅད་དུ། །
སྐྱབས་གཅིག་དམ་པ་ཁྱེད་དང་མི་འབྲལ་ཞིང་། །
བྱང་ཆུབ་ཐོབ་ཀྱང་རིགས་ཀྱི་བདག་པོ་རུ། །
གྱུར་ནས་འགྲོ་ཁམས་དོང་ནས་སྤྲུགས་པར་ཤོག །

In brief, in the present and in all future lifetimes,
may I never be separated from you, my sole protector.
May I attain enlightenment and become the lord of the
lineage
and empty the city of cyclic existence of the six realms.

This prayer was improvised by Ngawang Lodrö Tsungmed right after a Vajra disciple named Khenpo Ridro sincerely requested a prayer to supplicate the guru to accept the disciple for all lifetimes at Mount Wutai.

༄། །སྨོན་ལམ་རྒྱ་མཚོའི་ཡང་སྙིང་ཀུན་བཟང་ཞིང་གི་ཉེ་མ་ཞེས་བྱ་བ་བཞུགས། །

བགྲང་ཡས་ཚོགས་ཟུང་དཔལ་གྱིས་བསྐྲུན་པའི་སྐུ། །
ཡན་ལག་དྲུག་ཅུ་ལྡན་པ་ཚངས་དབྱངས་གསུང་། །
སྟོབས་བཅུའི་ཡོན་ཏན་ཀུན་ནས་རྫོགས་པའི་ཐུགས། །
ཐུབ་དབང་ལྷ་ཡི་ལྷ་མཆོག་དགོངས་སུ་གསོལ། །

སྡུག་བསྔལ་གསུམ་གྱིས་ཆེས་ཆེར་མནར་བའི་ཚོགས། །
གང་གིས་བརྩེ་ཆེན་ཐུགས་རྗེས་ཉེ་བར་བཟུང་། །
དོན་གཉིས་འདོད་པ་ཡིད་བཞིན་འཇོ་བའི་ཕྱིར། །
བླ་མེད་བྱང་ཆུབ་མཆོག་ཏུ་ཐུགས་བསྐྱེད་ལྟར། །

Quintessence of Aspirations
The Brilliant Sun of the Samantabhadra Realm

Your body results from the merit of the twofold
accumulations.
Your speech is melodious with sixty facets, like Brahma's
voice.
Your mind is pervasively perfected with the ten powers.
Buddhas, the supreme deities of all, please be aware of me.

With great kindness and compassion, buddhas take care of
sentient beings tortured by the three kinds of suffering.
In order to fulfill the expected welfare of self and others,
I generate the supreme unsurpassable bodhichitta.

བདག་ཀྱང་མཁའ་མཉམ་འགྲོ་ཀུན་མ་སྟོང་བར། །
རང་དོན་ཞི་བདེའི་དཔལ་ལ་མི་ཆགས་པར། །
གཞན་ཕན་ལྷག་པའི་བསམ་སྦྱོད་རྒྱུན་བཞིན་བསྟེན། །
འཇུག་པར་བྱའོ་སྲིད་པའི་གྲོང་ཁྱེར་ལ། །

སྐྱེ་བ་ཀུན་ཏུ་ཡབ་གཅིག་མཁྱེན་པའི་གཏེར། །
འཇམ་དཔལ་དཔའ་བོས་དགྱེས་བཞིན་རྗེས་སུ་བཟུང་། །
ཀུན་ཏུ་བཟང་པོའི་སྨོན་ལམ་ལས་བསྟན་པའི། །
བྱང་ཆུབ་སྦྱོད་པ་རྒྱ་མཚོ་མཐར་ཕྱིན་ཤོག །

མ་འོངས་རྣམ་འདྲེན་དགུ་བརྒྱ་དགུ་བཅུ་དྲུག །
ཞིང་འདིར་མངོན་འཚང་རྒྱ་བའི་ཚུལ་སྟོན་ཚེ། །
རྟག་ཏུ་ཞབས་འབྲིང་ཉེར་གནས་མཆོག་ཏུ་གྱུར། །
རླབས་ཆེན་ཕྲིན་ལས་སྤེལ་བའི་མཐུ་ཐོབ་ཤོག །

Until sentient beings as infinite as space are liberated,
without indulging in the happiness and peace of
self-liberation,
adorned with the sublime intention and action of benefiting
others,
I enter the city of the threefold existence.

The only father of the wisdom treasury in all lifetimes,
Manjushri, the Warrior, graciously accept me as a disciple.
May I perfect all the ocean-like actions of bodhisattvas
expounded in the Prayer of Excellent Actions by
Samantabhadra.

When the nine hundred ninety-six future buddhas
manifest achieving buddhahood in this realm,
may I constantly become their close attendants
and attain the power to enhance their magnificent activities.

བཟང་ངན་ལས་ཀྱིས་འབྲེལ་བའི་སེམས་ཅན་རྣམས། །
ཚེ་འདི་འཕོས་ཚེ་བདེ་ཆེན་ཞིང་དུ་སྐྱེས། །
འོད་མཚན་སྟོང་འབར་གསུང་གིས་ལུང་བསྟན་ཐོབ། །
མཁྱེན་བརྩེ་ནུས་པའི་རྒྱལ་ཆེན་རྫོགས་པར་ཤོག །

དྲི་མེད་རྒྱལ་བསྟན་དར་ཞིང་ཡུན་དུ་གནས། །
རིས་མེད་འགྲོ་རྣམས་ཕན་བདེའི་དཔལ་གྱིས་འཚོ། །
དུས་ཀུན་ཡིད་ལ་སྨོན་པ་འདི་ཕོ་ན། །
མཐུན་འགྱུར་གསུང་གི་དབུགས་དབྱུང་དེང་འདིར་སྩོལ། །

May all sentient beings who have connected to me positively
and negatively
be born in the Pure Land of Great Bliss at the time of death
and attain the prophesy through Buddha Amitābha's speech.
May the might of wisdom, compassion, and power be
perfected for them.

May the supreme immaculate teachings flourish and ever
last,
may sentient beings enjoy benefit and happiness without
exception—
these are the only wishes constantly dwelling in my mind.
Please bestow the blessing of the assurance of speech here
and now.

བཀྲ་ཤིས་གང་ཞིག་ཕུན་ཚོགས་སྡེ་བཞིའི་གཏེར།།
མ་ལུས་སྐྱེ་དགུའི་ཉེར་འཚོའི་གསོས་སུ་སྨིན།།
མི་ཤིས་རྒུད་པ་བཙལ་ཀྱང་མི་རྙེད་པའི།།
དགེ་ལེགས་སྣང་བས་ས་གསུམ་ཁྱབ་པར་ཤོག། །།

ཅེས་ཡུལ་དབུས་རྡོ་རྗེ་གདན་བྱང་ཆུབ་ཤིང་གིས་བརྒྱན་པ། དེ་བཞིན་གཤེགས་པའི་ཁྲི་དྲུང་དུ་ངག་དབང་བློ་གྲོས་མཚུངས་མེད་པས་སྨོན་པ་དེ་བཞིན་དུ་འགྲུབ་པར་རྒྱལ་བ་སྲས་བཅས་རྣམས་ཀྱིས་བྱིན་གྱིས་བརླབ་ཏུ་གསོལ། སྦྲ་ཕབ་འཁོར་ལོ་ལས་གྲུས་སྐྱོབ་བསོད་དར་རྒྱས་ནས་དེ་ལྟར་སྨོན་བཞིན་ཡི་གེར་བཀོད་པ་དགེའོ། །རབ་བྱུང་བཅུ་བདུན་པའི་ལྕགས་རྟ་ཟླ་༩་ཚེས་༡༠་ལ། སྤྱི་ལོ་༡༩༩༠་ཟླ་༡༡་པའི་ཚེས་༢༩་ལའོ།། །།

May the nourishment of the spiritual life of all sentient
beings
and any of the four-qualitied treasury[2] ripen.
May the prosperous rays free from
all misfortune and decline pervade the three realms.

This was said by Ngawang Lodrö Tsungmed in front of the Bodhi-tree ornamented throne of the Buddha at Bodhgaya—the Central Land. May buddhas and bodhisattvas bless all to accomplish this aspiration. The disciple Sodargye transcribed the poem from the audio record and made the same aspiration. Excellent! The tenth day and the ninth month of the iron-horse year (November 29, 1990).

Part 2.

Teachings

1. The Supremeness of Sacred Larung

Section 1. *The Blessed Sacred Place*

As we can imagine, a supreme place such as Larung Gar Buddhist Institute is extremely rare.

The first Kyabjé Düdjom Rinpoché is a genuine embodiment of the wrathful emanation of Guru Rinpoché. His eight sons are the genuine emanations of the eight great bodhisattvas, and the life story of each of his accomplished sons could indeed arouse faith in anyone who has not yet gained faith and make anyone who has already gained faith shed tears. Among the disciples of direct transmission by Kyabjé Düdjom Rinpoché, thirteen rainbow-body accomplishers have welled up.

Larung, this sacred place, was blessed by these accomplishers.

Section 2. *The Prophesied Sacred Place*

When the first Kyabjé Düdjom Rinpoché was eight or nine years old, a Dharma protector, the red-black Shanpa Raksha, gave him a tamarisk arrow and told him: "In a future rabbit year, if you insert this arrow in the valley up there, retinues, disciples, and fame will all be perfected."

Later on, when Kyabjé Düdjom Rinpoché resided in Yangdrug, Dakini Gathering Monastery, all the dakinis also prophesied in the same way.

Therefore, after scrutinizing dependent origination, he told his retinue: "Today you guys go find some stones with different shapes and bring them back to me. They will reveal information about where I will live in the future." Afterward he obtained an ear-shaped stone, which indicated that it was best for him to go to a place that he had not yet been but had only heard of.

Later on the tantra protector Ekajata also prophesied that if he lived in the valley of Larung Yarchen, his disciples of direct transmission and lineage disciples would increase and perfect.

SECTION 3. *The Sacred Place That Enhances Realization*

A supreme place such as Larung is so rare that I have chosen it for my old age and death, still being able to make an independent decision. I guarantee that no place can enhance meditation experience or realization, or fulfill the activities of spreading the Dharma and benefiting sentient beings, better than Larung. Thinking so, I made the above aspiration.

Since you have resided in this sacred place, you should know its extraordinariness as well. Just as Guru Rinpoché said, to practice in an ordinary place for one year is not as good as to practice in a sacred place for just one day. To practice in an ordinary cave or under an ordinary tree for one year cannot realize the same blessing as practicing for just one day in a place blessed by the second Buddha, Orgyan Padmasambhava.

SECTION 4. *The Pure Sacred Place*

Larung, this sacred place, had not been defiled even during the Chinese Democratic Revolution and Cultural Revolution. In a word, Larung is a pure place, a place of blessing, a place of many prophecies.

Since you have already been residing at this sacred place, exhort yourself to quit all distractions and practice earnestly!

SECTION 5. *The Sacred Place Where Rainbow Bodies Were Accomplished*

This sacred place is where thirteen rainbow-body accomplishers appeared and where the eight bodhisattvas were born. It is an immaculate place, having never been defiled by the curse or misfortune of breaking tantric vows. Once I leave this world, you should continue living in Larung. Do not doubt it.

In the future, always remember this sacred place and me, your old father!

2. Listening to and Teaching the Sublime Dharma

Section 6. *Behavior when First Generating Bodhichitta*

Our Guide, the compassionate and skillful Buddha, said: "Listen attentively and engrave it in your heart, I am going to give you the teaching." You should thus carefully adjust your behavior when listening to a teaching.

The teaching that we listen to follows.

Now, both guru and students need to deeply ponder the fact that we have obtained the precious human existence so difficult to find, we have met the spiritual teacher so hard to encounter, and, above all, we have met the sublime Dharma, especially its quintessence, Vajrayāna, which is even harder to come across. At this point, we must practice the authentic instructions seriously, not wasting this human body endowed with freedoms and advantages.

If we fail to accomplish the true value of the freedoms and advantages of this human body on which we are relying in this life, we are bound to be impelled by the wind of karma into samsara in future lives. Having taken birth in the three lower realms, we could not be rescued even by buddhas or bodhisattvas and, due to the power of our karma, would not be able to hear the names of the higher realms. Therefore, from the very beginning, we should tame our mindstream with the four thoughts that turn the mind from samsara. Just as Bodhisattva Śāntideva said in *The Bodhisattva's Way of Life*:

> Leisure and endowment are very hard to find,
> and since they accomplish what is meaningful for
> humanity,
> if I do not take advantage of them now,
> how will such a perfect opportunity come about again?

SECTION 7. *Behavior before and after a Dharma Teaching*

The merit of listening to or teaching the sublime Dharma is incomparable among all the worldly virtuous deeds. At the start of listening or teaching, it is indispensable to pay homage to one's guru and deity. Reciting the homage prayer at the beginning of events like oral exams is also recommended.

As for the necessity of the homage prayer, that is clearly expounded in many commentaries. For myself, at the beginning of a teaching I like to prostrate to the unsurpassed King of Subduers—the Buddha—to demonstrate that I am a follower of the Buddha and to recollect his kindness. Since there are many followers of the Buddha, in order to show that I am a lineage disciple of the second Buddha—Orgyan Padmasambhava—I also prostrate to Padmasambhava. And among the many followers of Padmasambhava, in order to indicate that I am a follower of the omniscient Longchenpa, the great lineage holder of the secret Nyingtig (Heart Essence) tradition, I prostrate to the omniscient guru Longchenpa as well. Finally, since Longchenpa has many followers, and among them the only Lord of Buddha families—the omniscient Mipham Rinpoché's realization of mind transmission—entered into my mind and bestowed his essential points of profound instructions into the center of my heart, so to him, my guru Rinpoché, I also make prostrations.

Alternatively, we can also make prostrations in the order of the closely transmitted blessings. Today the Lord of Buddhism is only the kind guide—Buddha Shākyamuni. The foremost successor of his secret intention that he prophesied and praised is solely Padmasambhava. The successor of the most secret Heart Essence lineage that the buddha father and mother of Padmasambhva had directly accepted is the omniscient guru Longchenpa alone. And the most important disciple who had accomplished realization through Longchenpa's mind transmission is Mipham Rinpoché. Every little bit of faith, every bit of compassion in my mindstream, is definitely the result of the dominant condition—the kindness of Mipham Rinpoché either directly or indirectly. Hereby the order of the realization of the lineage.

Moreover, it is vital to remind the audience to generate bodhichitta. Just as Patrul Rinpoché once said: "The superior should remember to generate bodhichitta when they are leaving home for the assembly hall, the middling should remember it when they hear a Dharma conch blown, and the inferior should make efforts to generate bodhichitta when the guru reminds them of it." Therefore when giving teachings Dharma instructors should remind the audience to generate bodhichitta—this is crucial.

The daily chanting prayers we have been using are all from the tradition of Venerable Jigme Gyalwai Nyugu, except for the *Prayer to the Eight Auspicious Ones*, *The Prayer That Magnetizes All That Appears and All That Exists*, the Seven Branches of Offering in the *King of Prayers*, the *Taking Bodhisattva Vow Sādhana* in the daily opening prayer, and the aspiration part in the *King of Prayers* in the daily closing prayer. Personally, since I studied in the mountain solitude of Cangma Dzatod, no matter what teachings I give, advanced or basic, I always follow this tradition without exception. When you recite the daily prayers, it is better to chant from the *Eight Auspicious Ones* to the aspiration part in the *King of Prayers* without interruption or truncation. The chanting before and after teachings alone is of inconceivable merit. The compassionate Buddha expounded various kinds of inconceivable Dharma according to the different elements (*dhatu*), capacities, devotion, and intentions of sentient beings, but to follow the prayers is mainly for the benefit of people with middling and inferior intelligence.

For practitioners with superior intelligence, the only skillful means that can take one to the happy fruition of buddhahood through the happy path of bodhisattvayāna is this precious bodhichitta. As it was said by Śāntideva in *The Bodhisattva's Way of Life*:

Just as a flash of lightning on a dark, cloudy night
for an instant brightly illuminates all,
likewise in this world, through the might of Buddha,
a wholesome thought strikes rarely and transiently.

Section 8. *Bodhichitta— The Source of Happiness and Benefits*

This precious bodhichitta, this wish-fulfilling jewel, is the source of all the good things of samsara and nirvana, and the only cause for all happiness and benefits. With this precious bodhichitta, we can eradicate the suffering of all sentient beings in the three realms without exception. It can easily help us collect the accumulations for all happiness and virtue. This was concluded by compassionate buddhas and bodhisattvas after having scrutinized and examined for eons. Nothing else's merit can surpass that of bodhichitta. Just as Śāntideva said:

All the buddhas who have contemplated for many eons
have seen it to be beneficial;
for by it the limitless masses of beings
will quickly attain the supreme state of bliss.

Those who wish to destroy the many sorrows of (their)
conditioned existence,
those who wish (all beings) to experience a multitude of
joys,
and those who wish to experience much happiness,
should never forsake the awakening mind.

If this precious bodhichitta arises in one's mindstream just one time, this person would attain the title Child of the Buddha and become a bodhisattva. Just as Śāntideva said:

> The moment an awakening mind arises
> in those fettered and weak in the jail of cyclic existence,
> they will be named a Child of the Sugatas,
> and will be revered by both humans and gods of the world.

SECTION 9. *Bodhichitta with Inexhaustible Virtuous Roots*

Virtuous roots that are not imbued with bodhichitta would easily be destroyed by the four causes to ruin virtuous roots, such as no dedication or wrong dedication. Virtuous roots that are imbued with bodhichitta, even if they are the least significant, can bring us inconceivable happiness and the wealth of men and gods both in the short term and in the long run, before we reach full enlightenment. These virtuous roots will keep growing without exhaustion. Just as stated in *The Bodhisattva's Way of Life*:

> All other virtues are like plantain trees,
> for after bearing fruit, they simply perish.
> Yet the perennial tree of the awakening mind
> unceasingly bears fruit and thereby flourishes without end.

SECTION 10. *The Bodhichitta That Destroys Grave Misdeeds*

Moreover, if bodhichitta arises in one's mindstream, even the five heinous actions,[3] which can make the doer suffer immensely right after death, could basically be purified with no residue. Even if a little misdeed does remain, the person need suffer in a hell realm for only as briefly as it takes for a yarn-ball to bounce back up from the ground. As Śāntideva said:

> Like entrusting myself to a brave man when greatly
> afraid,
> by entrusting myself to this (awakening mind) I shall be
> swiftly liberated,
> even if I have committed extremely unbearable wrongs.
> Why then do the conscientious not devote themselves to
> this?
>
> Just like the fire at the end of an age,
> the awakening mind instantly consumes all great
> wrongdoing.
> Its unfathomable advantages were taught
> to the disciple Sudhana by the wise Lord Maitreya.

The first chapter of *The Bodhisattva's Way of Life* concisely explains the good qualities and benefits of the awakening mind, while detailed elaboration can be found in *The Avataṃsaka Sūtra*, in which over 230 metaphors were used to expound this topic extensively. Thus it is necessary to refer to *The Avataṃsaka Sūtra*.

SECTION 11. *The Bodhichitta with Ever-Growing Virtuous Roots*

This precious bodhichitta is of two types: aspiration bodhichitta and action bodhichitta. It is of foremost importance to understand the difference between their benefits and take the bodhisattva vow according to the liturgy. Once bodhichitta arises in one's mindstream, the virtuous roots will ceaselessly grow. This principle has also been said in *The Bodhisattva's Way of Life*:

> From that time hence,
> even while asleep or unconcerned,
> a force of merit equal to the sky
> will perpetually ensue.

SECTION 12. *Avoid Whispering to Anyone while Listening to a Dharma Teaching*

When listening to a teaching, advanced or basic, you should never whisper to another person unless it is about something extremely important. Otherwise the interruption will cause bleeding in the dharmakāya of a buddha, which is the gravest of the five heinous actions. If you wish to be born in any of the lower realms, such as the unintermittent hells, you are guaranteed to go there if you whisper to interrupt a Dharma teaching. However, perhaps nobody is willing to be born there.

I have repeatedly exhorted Dharma instructors to say nothing else while chanting the Eight Auspicious Ones until they have finished the dedication verses. If they indeed have difficulty avoiding talk, they should at least not utter any unrelated words over the course of chanting. This needs to be emphasized, and if it is frequently said, people will naturally remember.

SECTION 13. *The Benefit of Coming to the Assembly Hall to Listen to a Dharma Teaching*

Even if you are eighty years old, have the determination to attend Dharma teachings. Even if you have only five or six months left, you should still come to the assembly hall and listen to the teaching on the scene.

Old people, do not be lazy! If your condition is really bad and you cannot come, it is fine to listen to the radio broadcast of the teaching at home, but never give up coming to the assembly hall when you encounter only small difficulties.

You should all come to the assembly hall for Dharma teachings. The Buddha stated in many scriptures: "The merit of making offerings to buddhas and bodhisattvas, as many as the number of the sand grains in Ganges River, is not as great as that of making seven steps in the direction of seeking the Dharma."

SECTION 14. *It's Not the Same to Listen in Different Places*

Some people may think: "Listening there or here is the same. As long as I can hear the teaching at home, isn't it the same?"

As a matter of fact, it is not the same. As it is said in *The Jataka Stories*: "Sitting at the lowest place in a meek manner, looking at the teacher with joyful eyes, and listening to the teaching attentively is like drinking the ambrosia of speech." One should sit in a position lower than the teacher, carefully and strictly watching one's acts of body, speech, and mind, and with smile, direct one's gaze to the face of the teacher.

Of course, for people like me, smiling or not, the eyes cannot focus clearly. But if the teacher does make you joyful and you look at him with an outer smile and with inner joy and faith, the merit is indeed inconceivable. And in this manner, even if you meet the teacher only once, the merit is immeasurable already.

Actually, because you can hear the teaching somewhere else does not mean that you do not need to come to the assembly hall. Buddha Amitābha has countless disciples, which is stated in a sutra in this way: "Even if the number of dust particles on Earth were countable, it would be extremely hard to count the first set of disciples of Buddha Amitābha." Moreover, even though each disciple can listen to Buddha Amitābha's teaching anywhere clairvoyantly, they all choose to come to listen to the teaching of the Buddha of Infinite Light directly. Similarly, every time our kind guru Buddha Shākyamuni turned the Dharma wheel, his Dharma sound could be heard beyond countless worlds, but since it is not enough to just hear the sound, other buddhas would send bodhisattvas to visit Buddha Shākyamuni to greet him and listen to his teachings on the scene. Therefore you should come to where the teacher is teaching to listen to the discourse.

It is generally accepted for very old people, especially old laypeople with severe illnesses, to listen to a live radio broadcast of a teaching. However, as for merit, there is enormous disparity between coming to the teacher and merely listening on the radio.

Even if you could stay at Larung Gar for only six months, make sure that every single class you attend is well started and well ended. Examine yourself in this way: Have you generated bodhichitta at the beginning? Have you recited the *King of*

Group photo with Kyabjé Jigme Phuntsok Rinpoche after an empowerment to the Sangha at Larung Gar, spring 1998.

Prayers while reflecting on its meaning as dedication at the end? Just by relying on this simple skillful means, you can free yourself from further roaming in cyclic existence.

3. The Subtle yet Profound Principle of Cause and Effect

Section 15. *It's Better to Go Begging if You Have No Money*

It is always a headache to discuss the properties of the Sangha.

The Buddha once said: "For those practitioners who keep pure precepts and have attained liberation, I give them permission (to accept offerings); for those who do not protect their precepts, I will not allow them to accept even the slightest amount of (offerings)." It is pointed out that if a person has pure precepts, and on top of that has also liberated his mindstream through practice, only then is he allowed to enjoy offerings—so not everyone is qualified to accept offerings.

If one does not possess pure precepts or the quality of liberation yet has to survive on offerings, one should nevertheless attentively chant dedication prayers to benefactors because, as it is widely said: "The capability of a monk who does ceremonies is all about his mouth."

It is very necessary to handle these matters cautiously,

including allotting the offerings received in the Prayer Offering Center. It is for you guys that I am bringing this up; if it were just for myself alone, it would not be an issue.

If you have not participated in the chanting but have received a portion of the offering, or even two, three, or more portions, it is equal to committing the karma that could keep you in the unintermittent hell for many great eons. So never, ever do this!

If you have no money, it is far better to become a beggar than to take offerings that you are not supposed to have. When talking about beggars, Jetsun Milarepa was a role model. It is reasonable for a beggar to go begging; nobody is going to criticize that.

SECTION 16. *Earmark the Fund for Its Specified Purpose*

If the beneficiaries of some particular patronage include lay practitioners, then lay practitioners should get their portion; however, if patronage is specifically offered to novice monks and fully ordained monks, then lay practitioners have no privilege to enjoy it. We can decide this issue through thorough analysis and discussion.

I am told that a lay practitioner group received some offering after they chanted prayers, but if they allocated the money, everyone would get only a very small amount, so they put that offering in a fund for releasing fish. But would this work out? Would this make their activity virtuous or faulty? This can only be ascertained by the Buddha and the Sangha, not anyone else.

In the collection of sutra stories called the *One Hundred on Karma* (*Karmaśataka*), it was stated: "If offerings received in summer are allocated in winter, or the other way around, and if offerings for the right side of a Buddha statue are used on the left side, or conversely, then even if conducted by fully ordained monks, they have to experience sufferings without liberation until hundreds and thousands of future buddhas appear in this world." These kinds of stories have been collected in many Buddhist sutras.

Therefore you definitely have no right to accept an offering meant for another. We must make sure patron offerings are given to the persons or causes intended. If it is offered to the Sangha, we give it to the Sangha. If it is offered with the particular purpose of releasing animals, anyone with basic intelligence would not dare to claim: "Let's use it to buy food for the Sangha instead of releasing animals."

If lay practitioners cannot decide on an issue, it must be reported to a Sangha of at least four fully ordained monks who can ascertain it with logic and rules, forsaking careless remarks, as if it were a business chat: "It's a good deal! It will profit us."

SECTION 17. *Give Up Taking a Penny Not Given*

Whoever you are, if you have skipped chanting prayers, avoid taking the offering for it; doing otherwise would break the fundamental precepts.

Never, ever take the possessions of the Sangha either publicly or stealthily. As long as you have upheld the pure precepts, at least for novice monks it is better to participate in collective chanting and in this way get your portion by the Buddha. If you skip the chanting, you should never take the offering; otherwise you are bound to fall into the Vajra Hell after death.

As to the offerings, even someone who gives it to the wrong person creates a grave fault, not to mention a person who should not get any but enjoys it at will. However, in regard to sick Sangha members, they are eligible for their portions. Not only sick people but even their caretakers should get their portions. Of course, except for those with severe illnesses, you should not appoint too many caretakers for one patient because it is not good to interrupt them when they are in the middle of receiving a transmission.

SECTION 18. *Do Not Beat Dogs*

Please do not throw rocks at farm animals and stray dogs!

I talked about this last year. You may think that I am too softhearted, which may be true because I do have heart disease. However, and I am indeed not pretending, when you hurt dogs it is basically no different from pelting me with rocks.

Of course, the Sangha is no place for dogs. They should not be brought to where the Dharma is taught. Whoever offers to keep these stray dogs elsewhere, our Sangha can offer them one hundred million repetitions of the mantra of Avalokiteśvara for each dog they take away.

Reducing the number of stray dogs here is a difficult task.

Therefore do not bring and feed dogs here. For the stray dogs already here, please do not beat them!

Children often feel heroic beating dogs, but as a matter of fact, the title of hero is not obtained through showing off one's power in front of dogs. Based on the superior criterion of the Dharma, a hero is one who bravely eradicates the enemy of afflictive emotions. From the mundane point of view, heroes are people who can destroy enemies, which is also exhibited in the spontaneous song by Minister Shanpa in *The Epic of King Gesar*. Thus I really wish you not beat these dogs!

SECTION 19. *Exchange Oneself with Others*

From now on, if you beat dogs, it is exactly the same as beating me.

Some monastics pretend to be heroic, so they throw big rocks, like raindrops, at dogs. This is really the end of my forbearance. It sounds like I am lying, but when you beat dogs anywhere, I do feel sharp pain in my heart here. I have the responsibility to protect them as well, so please refrain!

As to the householders from pastoral areas, they are beyond our control. They get used to beating dogs and we can do nothing about it, just as we can do nothing for sentient beings in the three lower realms who constantly experience unbearable sufferings. However, anyone from my retinue, anyone regarding me as his or her guru, please quit harming any sentient beings, especially these old dogs around us. Please! Thank you!

Indeed, sometimes when I recall the suffering of sentient beings in the degeneration time, ripened through the power of their karma, I feel so restless that I cannot sit still, and I feel even worse if I see or hear their suffering in person.

Think about each farm animal sent to a slaughterhouse. The suffering they have to experience due to their karma is indeed terrifying. They are purchased in pasture and thrown into trucks, their lips nailed shut because it is said they will not lose weight if they do not chew. The various sufferings they then experience in the slaughterhouse are not much different from the sufferings of hells, except theirs is for a shorter duration. Every time they come to my mind, I feel as if I were about to have a heart attack, but we could do nothing about their plight.

Section 20. *To Whom We Make Offerings Ensues the Greatest Merit*

If one's misdeeds involve the Three Jewels—the Buddha, the Dharma, and the Sangha—those misdeeds are the gravest and usually bear results in this very lifetime. Even if the results do not ripen in this life, they will definitely mature in the next lifetime after death. Likewise, making offerings to the Three Jewels, even a little bit, will cultivate vast merit as well.

Moreover, compared with making offerings to the Buddha and the Dharma, the merit of offering to the Sangha is even greater, since the Sangha is the collective embodiment of the Three Jewels.

If we make offerings to Buddha statues, relic stupas, and so forth, we accumulate the merit of offering but lack the merit of enjoying, whereas offering to the Sangha creates not only the merit of offering but also the merit of enjoying. Even if the offering is a modest sum of money, or simple tools, or one bite of food, the effects will basically ripen in this very lifetime. Moreover, the merit will not exhaust after it ripens in this life but will keep engendering vast fruits until one reaches buddhahood or full enlightenment.

The Jewel of the Sangha is the perfect field for accumulating merit. If you are able to offer your possessions, even a little, you can expect unexpectedly vast merit and benefit.

SECTION 21. *Accept What You Are Supposed to Get*

When allotting money from the Prayer Offering Center, our financial department should pay extra attention. I saw that you have not seriously read the allotting regulation. You'd better read it through carefully.

As for people who spend most of their time listening and reflecting diligently, if you don't have much time to chant prayers, the Buddha allows you to chant briefly. As it is said, "Even to offer everything in the three realms is not enough," meaning it is not quite enough to offer even all the wealth of the three realms to people who have upheld their precepts and who diligently listen to and reflect on the Dharma.

You should enthusiastically participate in any occasion of collective chanting. As I mentioned the other day, never tell lies when you claim offerings for chanting prayers, for to lie is to absolutely break the fundamental precepts, which generates a scary karma leading to rebirth in the lower realms. It is terrible for, first of all, it is stealing, and second, it is inappropriately enjoying the possessions of the Sangha, and third, it is swindling. We have to be very cautious regarding the possessions of the Sangha! Unless you maintain pure precepts and listen and reflect diligently, you should never enjoy offerings at will.

The terrifying thought sometimes occurs to me that for their entire lives some people live on offerings they are not supposed to have. If a misdeed relates to the Sangha, it is a grave misdeed, opposite to the direction of Dewachen. The question ensues: Will such people end up in the three lower realms? We should give attention to these matters while alive. Impermanent death may arrive at any time, and it is uncertain who will die first, the older or the younger, and the external conditions of death are also uncertain.

And then, what would be beneficial at the time of death? The answer is faith, compassion, and your meditation on the Great Perfection. Here is the Dharma that can prevent you from roaming in the cyclic existence of the three existences; nothing is greater than this. Everyone should make great efforts to practice diligently. No matter who you are, it is indispensable to do your utmost to practice this Dharma.

SECTION 22. *Disparaging a Great Master Is Also Forsaking the Dharma*

If one commits the misdeed of forsaking the Dharma, one loses the opportunity of liberation, so we should be especially cautious.

But what is the misdeed of forsaking the Dharma? First,

it includes disparaging bodhisattvas. Since we have no idea where bodhisattvas are, we have to be careful to everyone. Bodhisattvas could be monastics or laypeople, and we also cannot exclude the possibility of their existence as animals.

There is a story of a man who was about to visit Mount Wutai. Bodhisattva Manjushri asked him to take this note to the mahasattva Dashi:

> The Mahasattva Dashi:
> You have finished your activity to benefit sentient beings with this body, now it's time for you to head for the eastern Pure Land of Manifest Joy (Abhirata)."

When this man reached Thrintu, he could not find the whereabouts of Dashi from anyone. Finally a householder told him that his family was going to kill a pig and its name was Dashi.

That person thought, well, since the bodhisattva Dashi cannot be found, let me leave this letter with Dashi the pig. But when he put the note in front of the pig, it managed to open the letter with its snout and died immediately after glimpsing what was written.

Bodhisattvas like this one can be found in various species of birds and beasts. Bodhisattvas usually make aspirations such as "May I become a bird or a beast or a beggar in cities." Sometimes they also make the aspiration to become one who is praised, one who is denigrated, one who is sick, one who gives Dharma teachings, and so forth. And in some extreme cases bodhisattvas also wish to become prostitutes or butchers.

Therefore, strictly speaking, we should not give malicious names to or criticize any sentient being; to do otherwise could cause the misdeed of forsaking the Dharma and is quite dangerous.

SECTION 23. *Disparaging the Dharma Is Also Forsaking the Dharma*

The misdeed of forsaking the Dharma also includes disparaging the Dharma just because one cannot comprehend some profound Dharma, mistaking it for unauthentic Dharma and holding wrong views on it.

For instance, in order to uphold one's own tradition, having an attitude of clinging to one's own lineage and hating other lineages, one may say the views of new schools are unreasonable or the views of Kagyü and Jonang are irrational. These are all misdeeds of forsaking the Dharma.

Usually laypeople don't talk about it and it is monastics who like to comment in this way. However, in the past when the Sangha of the earlier and new schools were in disharmony, lay followers also committed the misdeed of forsaking the Dharma under the guidance of monastics. Therefore we should give up denigrating the genuine Dharma and lineages.

In this age there are so many treasure revealers and accomplishers, whether genuine or pretended. Since ordinary people are unable to distinguish the genuine from the pretended, it is good to be neutral, giving up assertions or refutations. As it is said in the *Ornament of the Great Vehicle Sūtra*:

> The flaw of the mind is that it is toxic by nature.
> Inappropriate even when directed at an unfavorable form,
> it is obviously so when directed at the Dharma one doubts.
> Therefore being neutral is preferable, for then there is no fault. (II.15)

4. Being Unbiased toward Any Religious Tradition

Section 24. *Religions Must Be in Harmony*

In this world there are four major religions—Hinduism, Christianity, Islam, and Buddhism—as well as countless minor religions. If there are conflicts within each religion and between religions, sentient beings are bound to suffer immensely. Therefore all religions should be in great harmony and avoid contrariness or conflicts.

Section 25. *Different Lineages Should Be in Harmony*

In Tibet, the Land of Snow, there are eight practice lineages and ten teaching lineages. But all these lineages uphold the teachings of the same guru, Buddha Shākyamuni, so all lineages should get along well and maintain pure precepts.

Monastics in particular should avoid blindly favoring their own lineage or, out of desire and anger, saying things like, "We are the new lineage, you are the earlier lineage; you are the

Bon lineage and we are the Kagyü lineage." Otherwise you will commit the misdeed of forsaking the Dharma, a karma leading you to take rebirth in the lower realms. We should not hold faulty views on any teaching but instead practice on deities connected to us with sincere devotion. These days, thanks to the kindness of some marvelous lineage holders, the situation in the Land of Snow has changed and conflicts among lineages have decreased, though they have not yet been uprooted. So different lineages should not fight endlessly.

I cannot think of anything better than all of us pulling together so that Buddhism is slightly benefited, purer, and improved.

To benefit Buddhism means to benefit sentient beings. In contrast, like some individuals in the past, compelled by desire and anger, some monastics confirm their own lineage and dispute against other lineages through refutation and certainty. This is absolutely unacceptable. Such desire and anger toward other lineages are surely the causes propelling a fall into the lower realms.

In secret Mantrayana in particular, this kind of behavior violates the sixth fundamental vow, as said in the tantras: "If one disparages one's own lineage or other lineages, one breaks the sixth vow." Masters of the past also said: "For to transgress the sixth fundamental vow is to disparage not only the entrance-level path of the listeners and self-realized buddhas, or the genuine path of Mahayana great path and so forth, but also the non-Buddhist path in the course of seeking the genuine path."[4]

Especially in the bodhisattva vows, disparaging a lineage is regarded as the misdeed of forsaking the Dharma. If you wish to take rebirth in Dewachen after death, you must be cautious because no other karma is graver than the misdeed of forsaking the Dharma in this way.

Meanwhile, as to lineage holders who have the genuine Dharma in their mindstream, if one fabricates some faults that they do not have or denies their excellent qualities, slanders them, or attacks them with malicious words, it is also the misdeed of forsaking the Dharma.

Section 26. *Focus on One's Own Lineage*

As a Buddhist of any lineage, you should have firm certainty on the views and steadfast devotion to the Dharma and the deity connected to you. Obviously devotion alone is not adequate, so long-term practice is required. As for one's own lineage, whether it is the specific theories one learns, the sādhanas and mantras one recites, or the stages of the path and pith instructions one practices, one should know them inside out.

If you have plenty of time, you can study and investigate other lineages, but your focus should be on your own lineage. Guru Mipham Rinpoché said that he felt extremely fortunate to have been born in the teachings of Guru Padmasambhava and had extraordinary faith in this lineage. For myself, I was born in the Nyingma lineage and have focused primarily on practicing and spreading this lineage. On top of that, I have unbiasedly studied and spread other lineages and traditions.

Whether you are monastics or lay practitioners, you should avoid traveling around too much, visiting a variety of monasteries, or meeting with a range of people all day long; otherwise you will end up gaining nothing and wasting precious time in vain. Every individual should practice his or her own lineage perseveringly, thoroughly, and wholeheartedly. This should be the most important thing in our lives.

SECTION 27. *The Blessing from the Vidyadhara Lineage*

Generally speaking, the compassion of buddhas and bodhisattvas are not different. However, because of their different motivations and aspirations on the path of learning, praying to other buddhas over the course of many eons does not create the same power of blessing as praying to Guru Orgyan Rinpoché only once. Moreover, Rinpoché possesses the remarkable might of dispelling external disasters of earth, water, fire, wind, and so forth. This has been expounded in *The Seven Verse Prayer* to Guru Rinpoché, revealed by Rikzin Gödem (Rig 'dzin Rgod ldem).

Everyone should pray affectionately to Orgyan Rinpoché with strong devotion, sincere reverence, and above all firm conviction free of the slightest doubt. In the Land of Snow, it can be said that the perfect guru most closely connected to us is no one else but the second Buddha—Orgyan Rinpoché.

In regard to myself, in this lifetime I have been born in the teachings of the earlier translation Vidyadhara lineage and met with the Dharma of the luminous treasure of the Vajra. I believe that the blessing of the Vidyadhara gurus of the three lineages has dissolved into my mindstream, and I have fortunately attained mastery of the meaning of the Great Perfection. In general, this is all from the kindness of lineage gurus like the second Buddha, Orgyan Rinpoché, and in particular, this is also bestowed by the guru Mipham Rinpoché. Therefore if you want to receive blessing from me, you must rely on the teachings of Mipham Rinpoché, and as to the critical questions among lineages, you should never refute the views of Mipham Rinpoché even in a light and indirect manner; otherwise, the door to receive blessing is blocked.

For me, seeing even four lines of his words can enhance my devotion, compassion, spiritual experiences, and realizations and enable me to easily understand all the difficult points in every scripture. My mind dwells in such a state for seven or eight days. Therefore I hope you also pray to him sincerely and wholeheartedly.

SECTION 28. *Bodhichitta Arose at the Age of Five*

I have incomparable faith in the earlier translation lineage of the Vidyadhara, especially Guru Mipham Rinpoché.

When I was four or five years old, I recognized Guru Mipham Rinpoché as my ultimate refuge and prayed to him as a deity. My sincere devotion has never wavered and I always believed he and Guru Manjushri were inseparable, not only in their essence but also in their appearances.

To say I had this kind of devotion when I was as young as three years old is obviously unlikely, but surely I had it when I was five years old. I remember, once in my father's arms I clearly recognized Mipham Rinpoché as the lord of my buddha family, and from that day an uncontrived wakened mind (bodhichitta) arose in my mindstream.

SECTION 29. *The Profound Dharma That Should Not Be Neglected*

Right now we are in the age of degeneration of the view; usually in such an age the more profound the Dharma the weaker the faith of practitioners with small fortune. Perhaps you believe that instead of relying on a guru with Vidyadhara lineage instructions one can easily comprehend the profound Dharma through careless listening, superficial comprehending, and rough mastery of debating skills. If so, you are utterly mistaken.

Just as Guru Mipham Rinpoché has said: "Without the cause of ripening previous familiarization over a long time, even with a hundred years of assiduous contemplation, as well as great intelligence and diligence, one still cannot comprehend it." Therefore beginners who have just started to listen and reflect should never look down on the profound Dharma.

SECTION 30. *The Sorrow of Seeing Dependent Origination Being Ruined*

Initially I thought I had the past karmic connection of mastering the ability to reveal the cherished heritage of Orgyan Rinpoché—the eighteen hidden treasures, such as the profound secret mind treasures, the vast earth treasures, and so forth—and I am supposed to open the profound treasure gate, dispel the decline in the time of degeneration, widely spread the Dharma and benefit sentient beings, and fulfill the wishes of Guru Orgyan Rinpoché. It would be fantastic if one day I could join the assembly of dakinis and vidyadharas at the Palace of Lotus Light in the Auspicious Mountain, with the father and mother buddhas of Orgyan Rinpoché looking on me with a smile and joy and comforting me with the melody of Brahma, and properly enjoy the secret profound path of means, the path of liberation, and the Great Perfection, as well as attain a state equal to Orgyan Rinpoché.

However, since most dependent origination has been ruined, the profound treasure gates are tightened. Especially the dependent origination of unsealing the doors of the thirteen great hidden treasures has been destroyed, so all of these wishes cannot be fulfilled, about which I feel deeply sorrowful.

Section 31. *Comfort of Fearless Instructions*

When I was still little I thought to myself, I have been accepted by the iron hook of the great compassion and blessing of the earlier translation Vidyadhara lineage gurus, the blessing of the realization of mind transmission has entered my heart, and the meaning of the Great Perfection has also been mastered by my mindstream, so I will definitely attain the rainbow body and the accomplishment of luminous body.

However, since my illusory body has been defiled by some disciples' transgression of samaya, after I pass away, even if this body does not swell, it may not shrink. And yet even if it enlarges, do not doubt the Dharma that I have practiced my entire life or harbor faulty views. If you persist in your practice, even if this body swells, it will not do any harm to you.

As long as you sincerely view the gurus of the three types of kindness as buddhas, appropriately uphold precepts and vows, tirelessly practice the Great Perfection, and make the aspiration to be born in Dewachen, you will undoubtedly benefit yourself and others, and even all sentient beings.

SECTION 32. *The Harmony of Tibetan Buddhism*

In the past the learned scholars of Sakya, Geluk, Kagyü, and Nyingma debated wonderfully; however, some of us do not understand the necessity of debate and think that their views are completely contradictory. Whoever claims their debating is like the swordplay of incompatible enemies who cannot agree on anything is actually committing the misdeed of forsaking the Dharma, which can cause one to roam in the boundless lower realms.

As a matter of fact, all the Dharma teachings in the Land of Snow are the Great Vehicle teachings. When the Middle Way is discussed, everyone will uniformly agree on the view of the Prasaṅgika school. Nobody is going to say, I agree with the Svātantrika school. As for the Mantrayana, everybody without exception practices Highest Yoga Tantra (Anuttara Yogatantra). Thus it is crucial to understand that all the lineages are not contradictory.

Panchen Lama once said: "If all the Buddhist lineages are united, it will make a great contribution to Buddhism in its entirety, to ethnic culture, and so forth." Therefore among the different lineages we should not say things like "I belong to the earlier lineage, you are in the new lineage" with bias. If we jealously mock one another and commit the negative karma of desire and hatred, we destroy ourselves.

I am saying this seriously and sincerely. The different Buddhist lineages do not fall into "superior" or "inferior" categories, nor do they contradict one another. If you believe they are contradictory, it is only because you lack understanding.

SECTION 33. *Different Routes to the Same Goal*

In regard to the manner of teaching and expression, there are some differences between the Geluk, Sakya, Nyingma, and so forth. For instance, the new school holds the view that mind has to exist when one reaches buddhahood, otherwise there will be many faults in reason and logic—for example, a buddha would be a permanent and insentient entity. The Nyingma and Sakya believe that there is no mind at buddhahood, and they also have their supportive points for this view. However, no matter how different their claims are, they all want to express the same ultimate connotative principle.

What does this mean? None of the lineages—not Sakya, Geluk, or Nyingma—would say that the current dualistic mind, the mental factors as well as mental fabrications in our mindstream, will remain when we reach buddhahood. Moreover, all of the lineages would agree that every phenomenon—such as the wisdom, the ten powers, and the four fearlessnesses of the Buddha—can be unmistakably realized without confusion. We see, therefore, that whereas the conventional expressions and the scholars' specific teachings are different, their points of view are actually the same.

Whatever the phrasing in the teachings of all the learned ones of Sakya, Geluk, Nyingma, Kagyü, Drukpa, Dakpo, and so forth, there is no difference in their ultimate meaning. If you understand this, you will have mastered the fact that all the teachings of the various lineages and schools are not contradictory at all.

5. The Development of Larung

Section 34. *The Flags of Garuda Are Fluttering*

Now let me sum up. In the last twenty-one years, our Larung Buddhist Institute has had a variety of significant events. As I recently reported, on the tenth day of the monkey month of 1980, which is the monkey year in the Tibetan calendar, I arrived at Larung and founded the institute.

Starting from 1985, in order to revive Buddhism and bring unsurpassable happiness to sentient beings, we have spent a relatively long time in efforts to put things straight for a series of problems in Buddhism.

In 1987, the fire-rabbit year, the beginning of the seventeenth cycle of the sixty-year cycle in the Tibetan calendar, we, guru and disciples, traveled to the sacred Mount Wutai where the noble bodhisattva Manjushri resides and generated the supreme bodhichitta.

We have been working very hard since then to guide sentient beings of this world to Dewachen. In order to subjugate the demons and enemies who harm Buddhism and undermine sentient beings' happiness, we have been toiling tirelessly.

Finally, after all the hardship, we have gained complete victory. The symbol of victory of conquering in all directions—the flags of Garuda—have been erected in every corner of the world and are fluttering right now.

SECTION 35. *The Three Types of Equality*

First, equality of status. At Larung there is not the slightest difference in the height of the seats among all the resident monastics, whether they be just-arrived newcomers or top khenpos and tulkus. In the past when we held the ceremony for restoring vows and purifying breaches, we sat in an order based on how long one has been ordained; however, nowadays, because the Sangha has grown a lot, we no longer have that arrangement and everyone sits in an equal manner.

Second, equality of serving the Sangha. At Larung, no matter the kind of work, everyone without exception participates equally, whether the person is a gold-like khenpo or tulku with extraordinary wisdom, pure precepts, and virtuous character or a monk or nun just arrived.

Third, equality of financial support. In the past some monasteries traditionally offered gurus and khenpos and the like the same amount of financial support as offered to prayer-service participants, or double or triple their portions, even when they had not participated in the collective chanting service. This is completely unreasonable.

Since Larung Buddhist Institute was founded, I have never taken even one penny from the offerings for prayer services. Therefore you should carefully read the Vinaya scriptures. No matter who you are, great khenpos, great tulkus, if you participate in the prayer services you can take your portion of offerings; if not, you should never take any, for to do so is to make a big mistake with the property of the Sangha.

SECTION 36. *The Five Important Matters*

In this year of the dragon [1988]; the thunderous sound in the sky indicates the spread of good reputation far and wide. During such auspicious days, we should embark on our practice of magnetizing.[5]

Larung Buddhist Institute falls into four schools—namely, the monks' school, nuns' school, Chinese students' school, and lay practitioners' school. Of these four schools, the enlightened activity is magnetizing. From now on, Larung will focus on the activity of magnetizing, through which all worldly and spiritual goals will be accomplished.

As far as magnetizing is concerned, what indeed should we do for it?

The first important matter. When a flock of birds, for instance, lands in the same tree, it is impossible for them to live there forever. Likewise, everyone gathering here today does not have the opportunity to live in the world for an equally long time. Therefore, in this transient life, give up blueprinting meaningless long-term dreams. Everyone should give up nonvirtue and practice virtue, including making prostrations, circumambulation, accumulation of merit, and purification of obstacles, as well as generating the awakened mind. And then one should attentively practice the stage of generation and the stage of completion and so forth.

The second important matter. If you harbor hatred toward any lineage, that is an absolute cause to fall into the lower realms and is a misdeed of forsaking the Dharma, especially the sixth fundamental vows of the Mantrayana. Therefore the Sangha of the ten directions and the various lineages and schools should all be in harmony, uphold pure precepts, pay homage to the deities connected to oneself with reverence, and give up any hostility toward other lineages and cultivate pure perception instead.

The third important matter. In this present world, conflicts caused by desire and hatred, whether as serious as those between nations and tribes or as trivial as those in families, have taken place endlessly; we should pay close attention to this. To attain world peace, we need to work wholeheartedly to pacify and stop various wars and disputes between and among nations, tribes, and families; then we can create world harmony and peace.

The fourth important matter. All of you should avoid being jealous of people superior to you, stop comparing yourself and competing with people similar to you, and never belittle or disrespect people inferior to you. Everyone should do their best to cultivate a virtuous heart and engage in altruistic actions.

The fifth important matter. If the students of the ten directions of Larung Buddhist Institute as well as other people were all to practice magnetizing activities, that would be an extremely good thing, as such practice embodies all the enlightened activities. Relying on magnetizing activities, we will be able to realize the great aspiration of spreading the Dharma and benefiting sentient beings from now until the end of sky. As for the present, in order to take rebirth in Dewachen together in the future, we should all practice even more diligently.

Today, if any of you promise to chant *The Prayer That Magnetizes All That Appears and All That Exists*, come here to enroll.

For we are going to practice the activity of magnetizing from now on. We, the guru and disciples, make the aspiration together: "In the future we will come in front of Buddha Amitābha in person and receive prophecy to reach enlightenment from him. We will perfect our great aspirations, ripen sentient beings, perfect our pure land, and then benefit sentient beings until the end of sky."

Please bear in mind these five important matters. These are not instructions for monastic Sangha members exclusively but also my final edification to you, laypeople.

To summarize these five points, avoid any kind of dispute or conflict between lineages or schools, do not be biased toward any nation or ethnical group, and bring happiness and benefit to all sentient beings. This is the pure undertaking of Larung Buddhist Institute and worthy of being engraved in our mind.

Rather than keeping these words I just uttered a secret, you should widely spread them instead, for then you are my successors.

SECTION 37. *Practice That Is Suitable for One's Own Mind*

Whatever comes together is bound to come apart. We, the guru and disciples, are about 10,000 strong. We are like the flowers in autumn—how long we will remain in this world is unknown. Some people will leave soon and others will live together for a few more years, yet one day everyone here now will leave for the next life. When we die, besides the sublime Dharma, not a single word could benefit us. Therefore everyone needs to practice the sublime Dharma.

Of course in Buddhism the sutras are vast, the sublime scriptures are voluminous, and the knowledge is infinite, so it is quite difficult to practice the entire Dharma in our transient lives, especially in the time of degeneration when the external obscurations are extremely rampant. Therefore we must ensure that we practice earnestly the Dharma most suitable to everyone's particular mindstream.

As said in *The Dharma Song of Victory*, for the superior, practice the path of luminous Great Perfection and attain the fruit of rainbow dharmakāya; for the middling, practice all the Dharma treasure of the path of bodhisattvas and reach buddhahood step by step through the five paths and ten stages; and for the inferior, at least uphold pure discipline aroused through the mind of renunciation and be freed from all the sufferings of samsara.

SECTION 38. *Make Your Life Meaningful*

For those who have fortunate connection, focus on practicing the luminous Great Perfection on the basis of carefully maintaining one of the precepts. The Great Perfection can liberate us through seeing, hearing, and touching it. If you had a previous connection with it, even if you do not have the chance to practice it in this life, you can still attain the perfect unsurpassable enlightenment. Therefore everyone should do their best to connect positively with this supreme practice.

When favorable conditions are present we should not deceive ourselves. At the time of death, if you have the thought "it is no matter that I did an advanced practice or an insignificant one, I have exerted myself to my full strength my entire life anyway," then it indicates that your life is meaningful. Please bear this in your mind.

Kyabjé Jigme Phuntsok Rinpoche giving an empowerment of the Great Perfection at Larung Gar in 1984.

6. The Profound Dharma Gatherings

Section 39. *The Great Dharma Gathering of 100,000 Vidyadharas*

The main reason to hold the 100,000 Vidyadhara Dharma gathering is as follows: According to the prophecy of the *Dra Talgyur Root Tantra*,[6] "afterward, the wise will accept"—that is, if we hold the Dharma gathering of 100,000 Vidyadharas, all 100,000 members of the assembly can reach the state of Vidyadhara at the same time.

Initially, such dependent origination has already presented. However, due to the small fortune of sentient beings supposed to be tamed in the current age and the strong force of demonic obscurations, the dependent origination could not be completely perfected, which spoiled the dependent origination for opening the gate of the thirteen great hidden treasures. Nevertheless, thanks to the care of people from different backgrounds, mainly the great lineage holders and masters, in the Land of Snow we have the chance to hold this 100,000 Vidyadhara Dharma gathering after extensive rituals of recitation, supplication, and aspirations. In this Dharma gathering, we have over 38,000 Sangha members on the scene for sure, and to add other tangible and intangible Vidyadharas, the total number comes to 100,000. This is truly worthy of rejoicing.

Our sole motivation in practicing the activity of magnetizing with the *Profound Practice Sādhana of the Nine Deities of Avalokiteśvara* is to spread the Buddhadharma and bring happiness and benefit to sentient beings in the Land of Snow as well as the entire world.

Larung's teaching system should exist for roughly another 300 years, as was conferred from the prophecy of Lerab Lingpa and the first Kyabjé Düdjom Rinpoché. Although many other Buddhist rituals could be performed for it, the most important thing is to practice the activity of magnetizing—the great Dharma gathering of 100,000 Vidyadharas. If this Dharma gathering could be held regularly and appropriately in the future, the teachings at Larung would keep flourishing for over three generations after I pass away. Whether the Buddhadharma remains for a long time in this world mainly depends on this Dharma gathering. Therefore everyone should place great importance on it and participate with enthusiasm.

Nowadays, although the Buddhadharma flourishes in Tibet, phenomena keeping us from being optimistic are happening as well—for example, the brutal actions of non-Buddhists from peripheral places or the slaughter of hundreds and thousands of animals, which directly contradict the harmless Buddhadharma and airs harmful ideas. Just by thinking about it, one feels as if hells had appeared in our human world.

Last year I taught in many areas of the four rivers and six

ridges in Dokham (Mdo khams) and emphasized restraining from killing at Mastod (Rma stod) and Golog (Mgo log). However, some kindhearted individual told me: "You'd better stop talking about it, otherwise I am afraid your life will be in danger."

In its origin, Buddhism is a religion that requires doing no harm to any sentient being. The Buddha also said: "If you harm others, you are not a monk." However, the situation has already gone so far that people even doubt the dictum on no killing, and we are afraid of telling the truth besides. How can I shut my heart to ignore this and look on without lifting a finger? Therefore it is even more necessary for us to practice the activity of magnetizing.

Today there are about 182 countries across the world, but the Buddhadharma is nowhere as flourishing as it is in Tibet, the Land of Snow. If we reflect on all aspects, right now we are not yet in a situation of no protection from father or no refuge from mother, and neither is there nothing to place our hope on or nothing to rely on. And it is not a time that spreading the Dharma or benefiting sentient beings cannot be fulfilled. Quite the opposite is true. Therefore everyone should carefully and meticulously engage in these activities.

Today I vow in front of you guys as well. From now until the end of sky, in order to spread the Dharma and bring benefit and happiness to all sentient beings, even if I have to give up my life, I will never balk at the opportunity. Rather, I will fulfill the great cause of spreading the Dharma and benefiting sentient beings with my plan, and I ask you all to bestow favorable conditions of any kind.

SECTION 40. *Vajrasattva Dharma Gathering*

We hold the Vajrasattva Dharma gathering because we have accumulated all kinds of downfalls, especially the misdeed of breaking vows, and the most supreme antidote to purify them is the six-syllable mantra of Vajrasattva. It has been said in *The Wrathful Vajrapāni Deliverance Tantra* and so forth that if one recites this mantra 100,000 times, even the misdeed of breaking the fundamental vows can be purified. Therefore there is no need to mention that the obstacles to Dewachen—the misdeeds of forsaking the Dharma and the five heinous actions—can be completely purified in this very lifetime.

This Vajrasattva Dharma gathering is important for not only monastics but also laypeople. In the *All Lives Tantra*, it is said the number of mantra recitations should be 100,000, but "the required number of recitations in the Eon of Perfection needs to be multiplied by four in the Age of Conflict," so we need to recite it 400,000 times.

When chanting the mantra, articulation and single-pointed attention on one object are required. The superior are required to reside in the state of the stage of generation and the stage of completion. At the very least, one should recite the mantra with the four opponent powers. Reciting in this way, one will surely purify without residue all misdeeds—the misdeeds by nature, the misdeeds of breaking the precepts of individual liberation as well as the bodhisattva vows and the tantric vows, the obscuration of forsaking the Dharma, the five heinous actions, and misappropriating offerings.

The patrons of this Dharma gathering are the Vajra

Devil-Subduer District or the International Dharma Study Association. They are patrons because numerous Han Chinese followers will come to participate and also because this Dharma gathering is held during the most suitable season when it is neither cold nor hot. In particular, the postscript of the *Vajrasattva Sādhana*, the profound hidden treasure that I revealed at Lake Yutse (Gyu rtse), says that this liturgy will be easily accomplished if practiced near the place of hidden treasure and that it mainly benefits sentient beings in Han Chinese areas. Therefore I think it will be more beneficial to encourage followers in Han Chinese areas to recite the mantra of Vajrasattva rather than any other practices.

SECTION 41. *The Dharma Gathering of Ksitigarbha*

On this auspicious day, when our guru Buddha Shākyamuni turned the wheel of Dharma for the first time, our institute is holding the Dharma Gathering of Ksitigarbha, also called the 100 million recitations of Samantabhadra's Aspirations, but mainly the practice is on Ksitigarbha, since the 100 million recitations of Samantabhadra's Aspirations are generally practiced in all the four Dharma gatherings.

Like the Vajrasattva Dharma gathering, the Ksitigarbha Dharma gathering is aimed at householders and is specially arranged to ensure a plentiful harvest and to fulfill wishes. To reach these goals, it is not as effective to pray to Manjushri, Samantabhadra, Maitreya, Avalokiteśvara, and so on for many eons as it is to pray to Ksitigarbha for a brief moment.

This was stated in *In Praise of Ksitigarbha* by the compassionate Buddha Shākyamuni rather than by anyone else.

For goals as elevated as reaching the highest attainment of buddhahood, as well as ordinary goals such as bountiful food, drink, and clothing, and for good luck and fulfilling wishes, there is no better object to pray to than Ksitigarbha.

As laymen and laywomen, you must realize the good effects of praying to Bodhisattva Ksitigarbha. For instance, as we know, Sêrtar and its downstream regions, such as Drango, Doba, Nyarong, Garzê, and so on, underwent severe drought for dozens of days. During the worst few days, all the Sangha members of our institute recited the name of Bodhisattva Ksitigarbha and rain started right away. The prayer had such an immediate effect of blessings.

Supplicate Bodhisattva Ksitigarbha—your prayer will effect a long life, health, and riches. Prayer can also fulfill your wishes in this life and, in regard to the next life, is an extraordinary immediate cause for taking rebirth in Dewachen right after death, not only for yourself but also for sentient beings connected to you.

Moreover, ultimately speaking, if you pray to Bodhisattva Ksitigarbha, you will surely attain the supreme merit and wisdom of the hearers, self-realized buddhas, bodhisattvas, and buddhas. Bodhisattva Ksitigarbha is a unique jewel with whom even 100,000 wish-fulfilling jewels cannot compare. If you pray to an ordinary wish-fulfilling jewel, it can bestow only worldly wealth but will not bestow supramundane merit such as discipline, concentration, and wisdom.

Today we have this Dharma gathering. Our goal is to help

sentient beings in the Land of Snow as well as those in cyclic existence, and especially neighboring benefactors for whom we hold deep gratitude. Help them not only to have bountiful food and clothing, good luck and smooth sailing, but also to have no jealousy toward superiors, no competition with peers, and no insults toward inferiors. And finally help them to be free from hatred and all sorts of sufferings both in this life and when reborn in the lower realms as hungry ghosts and so on after their death. So it is to perfect their wealth and enjoyment and to shut the door to the lower realms for them that we have this Dharma gathering.

SECTION 42. *The Dharma Gathering of Dewachen*

We hold the Dharma Gathering of Dewachen on the day when Buddha Shākyamuni descended from Tushita Heaven. Farmers have harvested their crops, herdsmen are not very busy, and it is a relatively leisurely time for other followers as well. The reason we hold this Dharma gathering is that, relying on the power of motivation and the aspiration of Buddha Amitābha, it is easy for us to cultivate the aspiration to be born in Dewachen through practice and finally to actually be born there, so the gathering has the greatest benefit and merit. It is for the sake of followers that we've opened this practice of Dewachen to the public.

In particular, to take rebirth in Dewachen the supreme approach is to collect accumulation and the shortcut among all shortcuts for that is to join the collective practice with a great Sangha of pure precepts and lineage holders. The venue for this Dharma gathering is the lay practitioners' district of our institute, and in future they will assume the responsibility of holding it.

The Great Dewachen Dharma Gathering at Nubzur (Knub zur) village, spring 1993.

SECTION 43. *The Long-Life Dharma Gathering*

Holding the Long-Life Dharma Gathering is not for my own long life; rather it is for the Buddhadharma to be spread unbiasedly in all directions and remain in this world for a long time, and so that all the lineage holders, and especially one particular great master, live long in this world. At Larung we earnestly recite the *Long-Life Sādhana* by Ratna Lingpa (1403–78) at least 50,000 times. The power of blessing of this *Secret Collective Sādhana of Long-Life Practice* (*Tshe sgrub gsang 'dus pa*) is greater than that of any other sādhana; it is also necessary for everyone to practice it so that our own practice will be perfected.

Tertön Ratna Lingpa is a great hidden treasure revealer who has never spoiled the dependent origination. When the dependent origination of his activities ripened, it manifested as follows. A man went to see him to return some money, bringing with him a pricey ceramic bowl worth one hundred cows. The man filled it with milk and offered it in front of Ratna Lingpa, who was sleeping. When Ratna Lingpa awoke, the morning sun had just risen, shining its pure light on the white milk in the white bowl. Through this, the dependent origination had been auspiciously perfected, which enabled Ratna Lingpa to complete the activity of spreading the Dharma and benefiting sentient beings in just one lifetime rather than the expected three lifetimes. The teachings of the hidden treasures revealed by Ratna Lingpa have benefited sentient beings broadly. Whoever practices his teachings has found them to be of great effect and immense blessing.

7. Dispelling Misfortunes in Spreading the Dharma and Benefiting Sentient Beings

Section 44. *Buddhist Ceremonies Dispelling Contemporary Declining*

In our daily practice it is crucial to diligently practice this supreme *Revealed Practice of Vajrakīlaya* by Tertön Lerab Lingpa. So far, everyone present has received the complete empowerment, oral transmission, and instructions. The superior should do intensive practice, the middling moderate practice, and the inferior small practice—no matter what, everyone should practice according to their own condition for at least three days. If this practice could be spread throughout Tibet, it would not only dispel degenerations like diseases, famine, and conflicts but also bring happiness and stability to all directions and fulfill people's wishes. It is a requirement for the Buddhadharma to flourish widely and remain long in this world.

Take myself, for example—as mentioned in my biography,

I have undertaken inconceivable activities with the tremendous help of Dharma protectors. If people with pure vows make offerings to Dharma protectors by chanting authentic Dharma-protector sādhanas, without the presence of iron smiths, widows, and vow breakers, the might of Dharma protectors does indeed manifest.

SECTION 45. *Buddhist Ceremonies Dispelling Unfavorable Conditions*

Young people born at the end of the Chinese Cultural Revolution have not experienced serious social and political upheavals. They have good worldly knowledge but no experience of sudden and severe dislocation. Who has such experience? Hoary old people living down from the assembly hall. We have personally experienced many kinds of movements, both mild and violent. Therefore when another grave one occurs, we have the experience to neither offend the superior in power nor lose our own position. If we tackle the situation recklessly, it is bound to ruin everything. However, if we just let deities and Dharma protectors transform the minds of the people involved, anything can succeed.

Therefore we should earnestly chant the *Prayer to the Eight Auspicious Ones* seven million times in these few days.

After these few days, it is said that the work team[7] will arrive. We should plan for their arrival in advance, prepare what we should do, how to behave, how to speak, and so forth. Otherwise, if we just follow the crowd blindly, pretending to be brave when we are not, our institute will be destroyed in a moment. Everything we have achieved in the past two decades will go down the drain. Therefore it is foremost for us to tune our attitude to the situation to a moderate degree, neither too tightly nor too loosely.

SECTION 46. *Life after Life*

In all my lives I have never been separated from Manjushri Guru—Mipham Rinpoché. We have spread the Dharma and benefited sentient beings in a variety of relationships—as king and minister, father and son, guru and disciple.

In the future, at the time of the Iron Wheel King of Shambhala (Rigs ldan Drag po lcags kyi 'khor lo can gyi dus), Manjushri Guru—Mipham Rinpoché—will manifest as Commander Senge Bumba (Seng ge 'bum pa). I will become General—the Vajra of Activity. In the past, at the time of King Gesar, Manjushri Guru was the minister Tsashang Denma Jangkhra (Tsha zhang 'Dan ma Byang khra), and I was born as his son Densé Gyuö Bumé ('Dan sras G.yu 'od 'Bum me). It was also said in some prophecies that I am the reincarnation of Tertön Lerab Lingpa and the embodiment of Manjushri Guru—Mipham Rinpoché—but I take those statements for special necessity, having no certainty about them. However, if I am said to be the reincarnation of Densé Gyuö Bumé, I admit it is true.

Everyone here watching the opera of Densé this time will definitely be born in the entourage of the Iron Wheel King of Shambhala.

SECTION 47. *Vajra Dance of the Great Bliss*

If *The Melody of the Great Bliss Vajra Dance* by Mipham Rinpoché could be widely performed throughout Tibet, all kinds of diseases, famine, and warfare would completely disappear in the Land of Snow and the sun of happiness would arise. It has such dependent origination.

However, when Mipham Rinpoché was in this world, the dependent origination to popularize this Vajra dance did not ripen. Afterward great masters, like Radreng Tré (Rwa sgreng Khre) Rinpoché, Lerab Lingpa, and so on, had *The Melody of the Great Bliss Vajra Dance* performed as part of a general Buddhist-celebrating ceremony in the Land of Snow, but due to the inadequate merit of Tibetan people it was not successfully passed on.

Later on great masters like the second Kyabjé Düdjom Ripoché also tried to spread this Vajra dance, but still, because the happy time of the Land of Snow had not yet arrived, the dance had not been popularized in the end. And now all the dependent originations have ripened and *The Melody of the Great Bliss Vajra Dance* has finally been widely spread.

Wherever this dance is popular will be quite auspicious and free from diseases; all the degeneration of the turbid age will disappear and all the mundane and supramundane virtuous accumulations will increase. As the text of the *Melody* concludes: "Laymen and laywomen should have faith in the Vajra dance and single-mindedly watch it." You should have full faith in the dance; the performance is both entertainment and practice. You, virtuous laymen and laywomen in particular, if you can persevere in performing the dance, it will bring immense happiness and peace to Tibet—the Land of Snow—in general and various regions in particular.

Initially, even if you do not understand the meaning of the words, it is still quite beneficial if you dance along to the melody played on a tape recorder. The Vajra dance has various poses and movements that were designed by Larung. You should enjoy it with faith. Anyone who sees or hears the Vajra dance is quite fortunate.

8. Mastering What to Adopt and What to Abandon

Section 48. *Can Monastics Accumulate Property?*

Some people think there is no problem with monastics doing business. In the process of doing business, however, one can easily commit all the ten nonvirtuous deeds. If you have a big business, no matter if you are a monk, a novice monk, or a layperson, you are bound to break the fundamental precepts. It is quite difficult to conduct business without violating precepts.

If you spend your entire life engaged in business, when you head to the city of Yama after you die none of your relatives can help you and none of your properties and enjoyments can assist you. At that time, the only thing that could benefit you is the sublime Dharma. What can definitely harm you are the nonvirtuous actions that will accompany you, bringing you mere suffering. Ordinary people cannot let go of their property. No matter how involuntary the action, they have no choice but to leave a will of their property in this or that way. They can do nothing else.

Therefore you should not accumulate too many properties. However, as we know, nowadays some monastics accumulate great wealth, and among them, the worse cases are imposters—fake tulkus. Monastics and tulkus should look out for themselves! It is more appropriate for you guys to earnestly listen, reflect, and meditate. Didn't Patrul Rinpoché say: "When they can just ride a horse, if tulkus unscrupulously enjoy black offerings,[8] they destroy themselves and others."

If you travel around too much with merely a tulku title, I am afraid that you may not be able to secure your precepts. As I mentioned yesterday, if you are not a genuine tulku but admit to being such when others call you a tulku, it is very possible that you violate one of the fundamental precepts. The defeat is of falsely claiming to have the higher qualities of noble ones when one is merely an ordinary human being and has no such higher qualities. This is a grave misdeed.

Tulkus should not enjoy offerings recklessly from childhood on. Jetsun Milarepa once said: "The vital sword of black offerings can cut off the life root of liberation." It is indeed black offerings that can cut off the life root of liberation. Only bodhisattvas with the sharp iron teeth of accomplishment in practicing the generation and the completion stages are able to chew the iron balls of black offerings.

SECTION 49. *The Language and Behavior of Tulkus*

As gurus or tulkus, if you are immoderately reckless, it is very possible to break precepts and vows. This means you may sit on the high throne and under the elegant parasol today, but tomorrow you could suffer a sudden, devastating decline. Nothing is scarier than recklessness, which can quickly pull you down from the throne and parasol. Little tulkus should be cautious and careful in particular. As the old saying goes, "Newborn ponies have to undergo hardship for nine eons; after nine eons they will become fierce horses." Therefore little tulkus have many unfavorable conditions when they are young.

In fact, as far as you are concerned, pure precepts are the foundation; on top of which, if you have wisdom and meditative concentration, that is supreme. Even if you have no wisdom or concentration, as long as you have pure precepts, since you have already been recognized as a tulku and have the tulku throne, nobody will say you are not a tulku. Even if you cannot manage to make progress, ensure that you will not degenerate as time goes on.

However, nowadays some people are incautious; after they break precepts and vows, they pretend and tell people that they have clairvoyance. I don't believe them at all. If they talk lots of clairvoyance, they might say something correct by luck—just as it has been said, "When you drink sour drink, your body is going to shiver." But there is another saying: "The authentic can stand trial, like a long valley; the fake will quickly be revealed, like the tail of a mouse." Meaning, if it is authentic it can be proved with time; if it is fake it will soon be uncovered.

Therefore it is a first failure if you pretend to have clairvoyance and tell lies to people, it is a second failure if you pretend to be able to reveal hidden treasures, and it is a third failure if you pretend to have attained accomplishments. If you want to attain the status of a tulku, no matter that people say you are a tulku or not, as long as you can uphold pure precepts, everyone including celestial beings will regard you as a tulku and venerate you as a merit field. However, if you do not maintain your precepts, even if you have a silver tongue it won't help. Idling without any accomplishment is just a cause for degeneration.

Young tulkus should always be cautious; it is completely up to you whether you want to be a noble person or an inferior one. What is absolutely going to drag you gurus and tulkus down? Young women! They are truly the genuine enemies of young monks. Girls can throw you guys down into inferior places, so you must be careful.

SECTION 50. *Limit Association between Monks and Nuns*

We have neatened the disciplines among monks, nuns, and lay practitioners in our institute, so now the fourfold disciples here should all be pure communities. Anyone who cannot observe the five precepts of restraining from killing, stealing, sex, lying, and drinking can stay here at most for only five days; they are not qualified to be residents.

You should attend to the discipline of monks and nuns in particular. You must think it over with a calm mind—you are here to pursue Dharma practice and to uphold pure discipline, and you should never let Damsi, the demon who tricks people to violate samaya, control you. I have exhorted you about this before.

Be wary at the initial stage when you find you want to look at someone of the opposite gender; if you are not aware of it and don't take great care, you may want to touch him or her. If you do not nip this desire in the bud, your precepts will gradually be contaminated and transgressed. Therefore monks and nuns should guard themselves even more strictly than before neatening and never violate related precepts and regulations. Once you break the fundamental precepts, you denigrate precious Buddhism, and nothing is more harmful than this. So you should really think it over, and if you find that you cannot observe the precepts anymore, go home by yourself as the condition leads you to do.

Section 51. *What Makes You a Good Person*

We have already obtained this human body, and as well as possessing it, we have fortunately become discipline and *pitaka* (Buddhist canon) upholders and members of the fourfold entourage of Buddha Shākyamuni. Therefore we should be scrupulous—as monastics or Buddha's followers, we should avoid harming any sentient being, from the higher life forms, such as human beings, down to the lower forms, such as ants and small insects. The Buddha once said: "Anyone who harms sentient beings is not a monastic." So please apply this precept to your behavior and actions.

Generally speaking, residents in our institute should welcome and accommodate newly arrived monks, nuns, and laypeople. This has been a tradition in our institute and is also what a good person or a Buddhist is supposed to do.

In brief, a person who single-mindedly benefits others with a virtuous heart deserves auspiciousness as well as abundant wealth. By "good person," we mean neither an eloquent person nor a brave man, because the eloquent and brave could also be bad people. In general, a person with a virtuous heart is a good person. Therefore it is essential for us to have virtuous hearts and engage in virtuous acts.

What does "virtuous heart" refer to? It is to pray to the Three Jewels with faith, to wish all sentient beings to be as happy and fortunate as oneself, to have this wish for every single sentient being. Examine if you have such a virtuous heart. Obviously virtuous acts are even more important than virtuous hearts.

SECTION 52. *Keep Away from Nonvirtuous Friends*

As far as every individual is concerned, it is critical to relate to virtuous friends. Patrul Rinpoché once remarked that if you relate to companions who have strong desire, hatred, and ignorance, you will become one of them; if you associate with friends who have faith and compassion, you will have faith and compassion. Before you realize the first stage of bodhisattva, it is your friends and companions that shape who you are.

No matter where you live, in urban areas or remote mountains and monasteries, first and foremost keep away from nonvirtuous friends. As a monastic, if you like to associate with a business person, it indicates that you will become a business person; if you like to relate to people who love reading, it shows that you will become a book lover; if you like to be with people who always meditate, it means you will become a practitioner; if you like to be with nonvirtuous friends, it demonstrates that you yourself are nonvirtuous.

To examine whether someone is a good person, observe his speech, facial expressions, and behavior and actions. If he spends lots of time with business people, vagrants, or thieves, it proves that he is a dishonest person who steals as well. Haven't we heard people say that such and such a monk was an honorable person but ruined himself after associating with a bad friend?

SECTION 53. *Relate to Virtuous Friends*

Although you must have related to nonvirtuous friends previously, what is more important is to associate only with virtuous friends and companions from now on. Just as Mipham Rinpoché said, "You should quit all forms of distraction. If you can't, then relate to virtuous friends who are effective medicine for you." Meaning, if you really cannot refrain from distractions, choose to befriend people who have excellent qualities and you will be edified by their good qualities.

Moreover, everyone should cultivate compassion and refrain from anger toward others, whether they are your superior or inferior. Even if we are not able to stop hating enemies, we should at least never harbor hatred toward Dharma brothers and sisters who are our close companions, like lamp light and lamp wick, until we finally attain enlightenment.

SECTION 54. *The Three Key Remarks*

Just as the *Notice for Neatening Buddhism* reminds us, the foundation of Buddhism is to observe pure precepts; the essence of Buddhism is to diligently listen, reflect, and meditate; and the fruition of Buddhism is to benefit sentient beings. There is no single Buddhadharma that cannot be included in these three points. Even if all the buddhas appeared on the same throne, they would have nothing else to teach. Everyone should therefore apply the three points to their practice.

9. Abandon All Nonvirtue

Section 55. *Killing Is the Gateway to Hells*

If someone kills out of hatred, she will go nowhere but the hell realms after she dies. Some of you believe that without killing one cannot survive in this life, but this is not the case. For instance, at Larung we have around 10,000 monastics and we have all promised to refrain from consuming meat during Dharma gatherings. Foregoing meat, we've eaten even better and more than before and never felt that we are going to die without meat.

Indeed, relying on the kindness of benefactors of all directions, our clothes are better and our food more abundant, with regular offerings of yogurt and meals. For the three months of summer and the three months of fall, we have meal offerings almost every day.

Section 56. *Stop Unwholesome Practices*

As practitioners of the Great Vehicle Buddhism, we should do our best to stop the unwholesome tradition of offering meat to monasteries, which directly contradicts Buddhism. In Sêrtar, relying on the kindness of Patrul Rinpoché, we do not have this bad custom, but it has been said that it occurs in other places.

Moreover, I was told that some people unconcernedly hand over bulls and sheep to butchers by the hundreds and let them take these creatures to slaughterhouses because they need the money to build buddha statues and stupas. If this truly happens, they are deliberately destroying the Buddhadharma. I believe none of you here has done this. It is absolutely unacceptable.

One thing needs particular attention—please, never make a living by killing cows. They have been so kind to us human beings. These creatures are not different from us; they have the feeling of pain and are afraid of death, as we are. These sentient beings are not our enemies. Cows have fed us and protected us their entire lives, so they are our benefactors and do not deserve to be killed or chopped to death.

Therefore I repeatedly encourage all monastics and superior, middling, and inferior people to quit harming sentient beings and never engage in large-scale slaughter. It would be a different matter if slaughter had been required by the government, then it would be inevitable—but this is not the case. Nobody is going to die if other sentient beings are not killed, not to mention decimated, and to kill even a couple of sentient beings is unacceptable. Anyone who cannot refrain from killing will undergo misfortune in this life and fall into the boundless lower realms after death.

Section 57. *Cows Superior to Mothers*

You should stop blindly killing and slaughtering these kind cows, whose kindness is superior to that of our own kind mothers. Farm animals should not be slaughtered! Wild beasts should not be killed! They are all innocent. Wild beasts living around us are all the reincarnation of our parents and relatives. Their proximity to us is due to their attachment to us—they lost the chance to be born as human beings so they were born as animals here because of us. Absolutely first and foremost, quit slaughtering and hunting!

For your sake, I repeatedly pray to you to stop killing, to quit hunting. I don't know whether it is meaningful for a person who kills farm animals and hunts wild animals to sit in a Buddhist assembly.

Take Sêrtar, for example, where most people live as nomads. As nomads, if you end the lives of all your animals, what are you going to live on? These farm animals feed us our entire lives. Nowadays some people say that they kill all their cows and sign a contract to make a living. But you may not be able to sign such a contract and end up begging instead, with a begging bag on your back and a begging letter in your hand. Think how miserable it would be! How can a person carrying less than ten dollars sign a contract?

Last year and the year before, I was terrified to learn that hundreds and thousands of creatures were killed every couple of days, their shed blood running like rivers. Today the situation seems slightly better, perhaps because the retail price of beef has not gone up or some such circumstance. If this is the case, it is great.

SECTION 58. *The Source of Happiness for Present and Future Lives*

In Tibet, where Buddhadharma is flourishing, what can be relied on is solely the Three Jewels. If you rely devotedly on the Three Jewels, you will be happy in this life and in all lives to come. Therefore from now on you should not kill or hunt. If you can remain resolute, you will be happy and fortunate.

Last year I didn't have the heart to see people killing animals and eating meat. I thought, "If they continue committing such misdeeds, would it cause a great number of people in Sêrtar and the vicinity die from famine or illness?" I could not bear it and prayed to Bodhisattva Ksitigarbha wholeheartedly.

10. Adopt All Virtuous Deeds

Section 59. *The Merit of Releasing Lives*

These days vast numbers of followers have promised to quit killing farm animals in three years. Such virtuous action is astonishing! Good children, persist in your efforts! Four or five years ago I dreamed of Thupga Yishin Norbü (Thub dga' yid bzhin nor bus), who praised my merit of protecting and releasing lives. His words must be the speech blessed by bodhisattvas. After I passed on his words to the public, tulkus and khenpos were so excited by this ambrosia that they immediately promoted releasing lives and abstention from killing. Just in this year Khenpo Tsultrim Lodro has had over 100 million big and small fish released, and in the past a few years he has had hundreds of millions fish released. This is not an activity for only a couple of people. Everyone should spare no effort to release lives.

In terms of secular virtuous root, protecting lives is of foremost importance. Therefore everyone should place great importance on it and release as many lives as possible.

SECTION 60. *The Merit of Prayer Wheels*

When you spend 30 RMB (about 5 dollars) on a prayer wheel, the amount spent is minor but the virtuous root is infinite. Please make offerings to have a prayer wheel of your own! Please make offerings to own a prayer wheel! It is not an insignificant thing. These prayer wheels are from pure sources and have been consecrated by a great number of monastics. Every penny offered to purchase a prayer wheel here has been collected in a fund created exclusively for making more of them. My good children, be of great fortitude! We are all capable of doing this. Let us make offerings to purchase prayer wheels and spin prayer wheels.

We should avoid spinning a prayer wheel when it is not held straight up, and we should not leave it on a bed or step over it. Place it in a clean place. Please keep in mind that these prayer wheels are Bodhisattva Avalokiteśvara himself.

SECTION 61. *The Merit of Reciting Sutras and Mantras*

We, the Great Perfection practitioners, should write *The Tantra of the Single Child of the Doctrine* with gold.[9] If you cannot do this, you should carry it always, in a size the width and length of four fingers, and keep it at your body temperature all your life. When you die, have it cremated with your body. Recite it once every day. Even if you have no time to recite other sutras, this tantra has to be recited every day. It is the principal profound practice of the ultimate practice, and even if someone could go to seek a Dharma teaching in a pure land, she could not find anything more supreme than this one.

In today's Larung, you would be hard put to find anyone who does not have a *mala*[10] in his or her hand. This is my contribution, but I am not sure you have acknowledged it. As long as you hold a mala, it indicates that you are a follower of Bodhisattva Avalokiteśvara. Didn't Patrul Rinpoché once say: "Chenrezi is the one deity who embodies all buddhas; the six-syllable mantra is the one mantra that embodies all mantras; bodhichitta is the one practice that embodies all practices of the development and completion stages.[11] Knowing the one that liberates all, recite the six-syllable mantra." Recite the mantra of Chenrezi! Recite the mantra of Chenrezi! Recite the mantra of Chenrezi! *Om mani padme hum!*

Tibet, the Land of Snow, was originally the land tamed by Bodhisattva Chenrezi. If you cannot do anything else, you should at least recite his mantra with a mala in your hand. Or else you can recite the mantra of Vajrasattva, Manjushri, or Guru Rinpoché. There is no difference, all the deities share the same essence. Nobody could fail to practice this virtue; if anyone says he is incapable of doing this, it is a sheer lie.

SECTION 62. *The Merit of Lamp Offering*

The merit of lamp offering is inconceivably great; it is the king of making offerings. In particular, through the interdependence of the rays from a lamp to the ten directions, ignorance—the root of all afflictions in our mindstream—can be dispelled.

There is nothing better than making lamp offerings to dispel ignorance. In the past, great teachers of the lineage masters of Kadampa, such as Potowa (Po to ba), Shyangawa (Spyan snga ba), and Phuchungwa (Phu chung ba), had never interrupted the offering of butter lamps and water in front of the Buddha statue above their pillows.

In addition, the poor woman Nanda (Ba snyen dga' mo) offered a lamp in front of the Buddha and made the aspiration: "Today, I, poor woman, have offered a small lamp to the Buddha, and by this merit may I have the lamp of wisdom to eradicate the darkness of ignorance of all sentient beings in the future." After making this aspiration, she left. That night all the other lamps went out, but her lamp remained lit until daybreak. This is an example of the might of lamp offering.

11. Cherish Our Cultural Heritage

Section 63. *Wearing Tibetan Costumes*

We should alter neither Tibetan costumes nor Tibetan customs, including the way we wear clothes, hats, shoes, and so on.

Nowadays some Tibetan people wear clothes of Chinese style and claim they are leather garments. I don't know what they are made of exactly, but was told the price is a few thousand RMB. The garments look like leather patches or paint-covered rubber; they don't look nice and won't keep you warm. However, these days people who follow this nonvirtuous trend are in great number, while those who adopt virtuous actions are rare.

As Tibetans, it is great to wear Tibetan costumes. The discipline division of the four schools of Larung should check carefully and regularly to see if anyone's clothes have any alteration. Among us, if one person wears unique undergarments today, tomorrow a lot of people would be sure to copy it, but we don't know where the clothing is made and it must be standardized. In regard to monastics, it is inappropriate to wear different sorts of undergarments, and you householders are not supposed to wear monastic robes.

SECTION 64. *The Excellent Custom of Tibetans*

Generally speaking, it is of foremost importance for Tibetan people to wear Tibetan costumes. Wearing the clothes passed on to us from our forefathers, we inherit the excellent customs of ancient times as well as the ways of the superior. Otherwise, if we alter our clothes and our language at will, the local deities, earth gods, and so on will be offended and they will create chaos, causing disease, famine, and wars all around.

As a matter of fact, Tibetans have unique characteristics. Beginning in the reign of the three kings of Dharma (*chos gyal*) of the Tibetan Empire (618–842)—Songtsen Gampo, Trisong Detsen, and Ralpachen (Trisuk Detsen)—Tibetan people established the tradition of holding malas and spinning prayer wheels, reciting the mantra of Chenrezi, and eating *tsampa*[12] with their hands. Tsampa is rich in nutrients—people who eat it feel easy and brisk when climbing mountains. Seeing a person holding a mala, people naturally ask: "What part of Tibet are you from?" Even if you cannot practice extensively, if you hold a mala, spin a prayer wheel, and recite the mantra of Chenrezi, you can be counted as a pure Tibetan Buddhist.

Section 65. *The Soul of Ancestors—Language and Scripts*

Never overlook the Tibetan language and Tibetan scripts! Some Tibetans appear to be able to speak Chinese and thus think of themselves as brilliant. They keep talking all the time in Chinese exclusively. They should not be proud of being able to speak Chinese. In the current era when Chinese is so popularized, almost nobody is versed in the traditional Chinese of a century ago. The structure of the characters has changed and stacks of sutras have been put on the shelves, just like piles of blank paper. In Tibet, from the Dharma king Songtsen Gampo until today, our handwriting scripts have never been altered, not even slightly, not one single script. However, it has been said that nowadays at some presses people add vowel marks below and above scripts. Even this kind of change is not acceptable.

Section 66. *The Characteristics of Tibetan Scripts*

Take Chinese characters. To understand Buddhist teachings, one has to learn maybe twenty thousand characters. Without mastering such large number of characters, it is certain that one cannot do a good translation. Without mastering several thousand characters, there is no way to do a translation at all. However, look at the Tibetan language. How many scripts do we have? Four vowels and thirty consonants. As long as you have mastered them, you can use Tibetan to teach the

Buddhadharma and communicate in daily life as you like. Tibetan scripts should not be altered! The Tibetan language should not be forgotten!

12. The Promise to Welcome the Fortunate Ones

Section 67. *The Excellence of Dewachen*

Every instance of pure discipline we observe, every virtuous deed we do, we should be mindful of dedicating it to be born in the Pure Land. Except for some special cases, we should have a fierce aspiration to be born in Dewachen—the Pure Land of Great Bliss. No other Buddha realms can compare with it.

To be born in Dewachen is very easy and of great merit. Relying on the power of aspiration and the motivation of Buddha Amitābha, except in cases of forsaking the Dharma and committing one of the heinous misdeeds, taking rebirth there is guaranteed. Although it is hard to avoid the misdeed of forsaking the Dharma, most of us should not have violated it so greatly as to truly hinder taking rebirth in Dewachen. As practitioners who have been listening to and reflecting and meditating on the Dharma, we should confess sincerely, try our best to purify misdeeds, and disclose and confess misdeeds with discretion. As for the heinous misdeeds, we generally do not commit them. So we should cultivate faith in taking rebirth in Dewachen and long for it.

SECTION 68. *Being Undistracted*

Initially when I made aspiration in front of Bodhisattva Manjushri at Mount Wutai in the Chinese area, my highest aspiration was to guide all sentient beings across the world onto the path of liberation, my middling aspiration was to lead most people in China on the path to liberation, and the lowest aspiration was to take the majority of people in the Land of Snow on the path to liberation.

Afterward, not only Tibetans but also a number of Chinese and people in other countries have gained sincere faith. This is truly the might of aspiration of Bodhisattva Manjushri. My wish is that can I make everyone who sees me, hears me, remembers me, or touches me take rebirth in Dewachen. If this is impossible, can most of them do so? Haven't I told you before? I myself make the aspiration in my daily practice to take rebirth in Dewachen. I hope you also make this choice.

Some people make the aspiration to be born in Tushita Heaven one time, then on Copper-Colored Auspicious Mountain another time, then in the Pure Land of Manifest Joy the next time, and then on Potala Mountain, and so on. This is truly not good. At the moment of death, our mind is in a state similar to a state of mind suddenly hit by a flash of lightning and a thunderbolt strike. If you cannot keep your mind calm at that time, first praying to Guru Rinpoché for a while, then praying to Jetsun Tara for a moment, then taking refuge with a guru for an instant, then taking refuge with the Buddha, and so on, without a determined point of focus, and just murmuring like a madman, how can you work it out or process the experience? The moment of death is extremely horrific.

When "Pure Land practice" is spoken of, this pure land does not require our own force of will, because Buddha Amitābha has already set up a sumptuous, palatable feast that is waiting for us. To be born there is just like a son going back to his father's house, not difficult at all. Therefore everyone should have a single-pointed intention to be born in Dewachen.

SECTION 69. *Taking Rebirth in Dewachen All Together*

Both Orgyan Padmasambhava and Guru Mipham Rinpoché said that I will be able to benefit vast numbers of sentient beings and help sentient beings who have a connection with me take rebirth in Dewachen. In particular, over two hundred years ago, a guru called Dodrupgen (Rdo grub rgan) explicitly prophesied that a holy mountain called Ngala Taktsé (Rnga la stag rtse) was below, a holy mountain named Damchan (Dam can) was above, and a tree goddess called Thong Ngu (Thong ngu) resides in a place called Larung, where four schools of Sangha members and I live.

In addition, Lerab Lingpa also said that in the place called Dzumed Cholha (Rdzu med chos lhas) there will be a person named Jigme Phuntsok; his father is named Padma and his mother Yumtso (G.yu mtsho); he will be born in the year of the rooster; there will be a variety of auspicious signs of his body, speech, and mind; and he will turn the wheel of Dharma to eradicate the decline of the degeneration time and lead sentient beings to Dewachen.

They all uttered this before I was born and they never tell lies. If this had been said after I was born, it might be taken as some encouragement from gurus, but that is not the case. There are also other prophecies. I am telling this to delight you, and not lying for my own sake. Therefore you should make aspiration to take rebirth in Dewachen joyfully and delightedly.

People who have gathered here today should all be honest and sincere, quit fighting and quit stealing. If you can do that, I believe each of you can be born in Dewachen without exception. As a person so close to death, the reason why I am still endeavoring for your rebirth in the Pure Land is because I believe these prophecies will not go wrong, and I wish to benefit vast numbers of sentient beings as well.

Therefore if you can recite the name of Buddha Amitābha one million times, you will take rebirth in Dewachen right after you die. I can secure this with the witness of buddhas and bodhisattvas, so you do not need to doubt or hesitate.

13. Final Advice

Section 70. *Last Will at the Dewachen Dharma Gathering*

Aspire to take rebirth in Dewachen and keep this in mind constantly; this is my first piece of advice.

Make great effort to stop killing any sentient beings, please, and thank you; this is my second advice.

Have a good heart toward everyone—superior, inferior, and equal to you; this is my third advice.

These three pieces of advice embody the entire Buddhdharma.

This gathering might be our last one, though I hope it is not. My wish is that we see one another again, and I aspire to meet you again in this life. However, it might happen that I will soon leave this world. If I die, you might say, "We should find his reincarnation," even within forty-nine days after my death. Without having enough time to develop in the womb for nine months and ten days, my reincarnation may still be recognized.[13] But if I have some control, I would not like to take rebirth in this world soon after I die.

I always think that after I die I will see Buddha Amitābha in Dewachen and listen to his teachings. He will gently put his lotus-petal-like right hand on the crown of my head and bestow the prophecy of my enlightenment, and then I will master the clairvoyance of superpowers. So that, if I can benefit more sentient beings when I come back to this world, I would not be as weak and helpless as I am now. Rather, I will have the mastery of wisdom, skillful means, diligence, concentration, clairvoyance, and so on because I will have the ocean-like merit. As is said in *The King of Aspiration Prayers*: "As I wander through all states of samsaric existence, may I gather inexhaustible merit and wisdom and so become an inexhaustible treasury of noble qualities of skill and discernment, samadhi and liberation!"

Out of compassion, I will never forsake this world, and the Land of Snow in particular, especially the downstream area of Dokam (Mdo khams)—my hometown Palshul (Bal shul) Sêrtar. Whatever pure land I take rebirth in, I will never forsake the land where I have lived, including the monastery and monastics and followers on this land.

SECTION 71. *Last Will*

Do not forsake your own path, do not disturb the minds of others.

This translation was completed at Larung on the seventeenth day of the twelfth month of the fire-monkey year (February 12, 2017).

Notes

1. "Pure land" or buddha field (Skt. *buddhakṣetra*) refers to a region offering respite from karmic transmigration. It is said to be a land of beauty that surpasses all other realms, inhabited by gods, men, flowers, and fruits, and adorned with wish-granting trees. In Pure Land traditions, entering the Pure Land is perceived as equivalent to attaining enlightenment. Upon entry, the practitioner is then instructed by Buddha Amitābha and numerous bodhisattvas until full and complete enlightenment is reached. The person then can return as a bodhisattva to any of the six realms of existence in order to help sentient beings in samsara or stay for the duration, reach buddhahood, and deliver beings to the shore of liberation.

2. The four-qualitied treasury refers to wealth, sense pleasure, sublime Dharma, and liberation. The first two are the cause and effect of worldly happiness; the last two are the cause and effect of supramundane happiness.

3. The five heinous actions are killing one's father, mother, or an arhat, maliciously injuring the Buddha, and creating schism in the Sangha.

4. Dalai Lama Yönten Gyatso (Yon tan Rgya mtsho, 19th–20th c.), *The Commentary on the Three Types of Disciplines.* (A popular two-part commentary on Rigdzin Jigme Lingpa's *Treasury of Precious Qualities*, called *Lamp of Moonlight and Rays of Sunlight.*)

5. The practice of magnetizing refers to benefiting more sentient beings by attracting more people to study and practice the Dharma, which implies the necessity of first subduing one's own afflictive emotions and becoming more steady and capable of benefiting sentient beings.

6. *Sgra thal 'gyur rtsa ba'i rgyud* (one of eighteen Dzogchen tantras).

7. The reference is to the work team sent to Larung by the government, and to avoid any trouble this is deliberately expressed in an oblique manner.

8. Offerings made to request the transference of consciousness of the newly deceased.

9. There is a tradition of writing the most precious Dharma text with gold powders.

10. A string of prayer beads.

11. The deity Chenrezi, the Tibetan Avalokiteśvara, is said to embody the compassion of all buddhas and is known as the Bodhisattva of Compassion.

12. Ground and roasted barley, a staple food of Tibetans.

13. Rinpoché means it would be a fake incarnation because it is too quick to be born in less than forty-nine days.

Works Referenced

Sutras, Tantras, Prayers, and Sādhanas

All Lives Tantra. Kun skyed rgyud.

The Flower Ornament Scripture: A Translation of the Avatamsaka Sūtra (*Avataṃsaka Sūtra. Mdo phal po che*). Translated by Thomas Cleary. Boston: Shambhala Publications, 1993.

In Praise of Ksitigharbha. Sa snying bstod pa.

The Long-Life Sādhana (*Secret Collective Sādhana of Long-Life Practice*). *Tshe sgrub gsang ba 'dus pa.* By Tsedrup Sangwa Düpa.

The Melody of the Great Bliss Vajra Dance. Kun mkhyen me pham rgya mtsho'i zhal snga nas mdzad pa'i gling bro bde chen rdo rje'i rol mo. By Mipham Rinpoché.

One Hundred on Karma [a collection of sutra stories]. *Karmaśataka. Las brgya pa.*

Prayer to the Eight Auspicious Ones. Āryamaṅgalāṣṭakagāthā. 'Phags pa bkra shis brgyad pa'i tshigs su bcad pa bzhugs so.

Profound Practice Sādhana of the Nine Deities of Avalokiteśvara. Gar dbar lha dgu'i zab sgrub.

Revealed Practice of Vajrakīlaya. Gter chen las rab gling pa'i phur pa dus babs kyi gter chos. By Tertön Lerab Lingpa.

The Tantra of the Single Child of the Doctrine. Bstan bu'i bklag thabs bsdus pa bzhugs.

Vajrasattva Meditation: An Illustrated Guide (*Vajrasattva Sādhana. Rdor sems kyi kha byang*). Khenpo Yeshe Phuntsok. Somerville, MA: Wisdom Publications, 2015.

The Vinaya scriptures. *Vinayāgama.*

The Wrathful Vajrapāni Deliverance Tantra. Phyag rdor drag po mngon 'byung gi rgyud.

Primary Sources in Modern Translations

Longchen Yeshe Dorje and Kangyur Rinpoche. *Treasury of Precious Qualities, by Jigme Lingpa. Book 1: Sūtra Teachings*. Commentary by Longchen Yeshe Dorje and Kangyur Rinpoche. Translated by the Padmakara Translation Group. Rev. ed. Boston: Shambhala Publications, 2010.

Longchen Yeshe Dorje and Kangyur Rinpoche. *Treasury of Precious Qualities, by Jigme Lingpa. Book 2: Vajrayana and the Great Perfection.* Commentary by Longchen Yeshe Dorje and Kangyur Rinpoche. Translated by the Padmakara Translation Group. Boston: Shambhala Publications, 2013.

Maitreya. *Ornament of the Great Vehicle Sūtras: Maitreya's "Mahāyānasūtrālaṃkāra" with Commentaries by Khenpo Shenga and Ju Mipham.* Translated by the Dharmachakra Translation Committee. Boston: Snow Lion, 2014.

Ācārya Śāntideva. *A Guide to the Bodhisattva's Way of Life = Bodhisattvacharyāvatāra = Byang chub sems dpai' spyod pa la jug pa.* English translation by Stephen Batchelor. Dharamsala: Library of Tibetan Works & Archives, 1979.

About the Author and the Translator

His Holiness Jigme Phuntsok (1933–2004) was a prominent teacher in the Nyingma tradition of Tibetan Buddhism who was recognized as a tertön and renowned for his mastery of Dzokchen and his visionary activities. Unlike many Tibetan masters who fled to India and the West, Jigme Phuntsok remained in China throughout the Cultural Revolution and played a major role in maintaining and reviving Buddhism in the region. He established the nonsectarian Buddhist community of Larung Gar near the mountain town of Sêrtar in China's Sichuan Province, one of the largest monastic settlements in the world and a vibrant Buddhist teaching center that has contributed enormously to the resurgence of Buddhism in Tibet and China.

Khenpo Sodargye was born in Tibet in 1962 in what is today the Sichuan Province of China. He spent his early years herding yaks, and after attending Garzé Normal School entered Larung Gar Buddhist Institute in Sêrtar, becoming a monk in 1985 under the great Jigme Phuntsok Rinpoché. Khenpo served Rinpoché as his personal and teaching interpreter on overseas tours in Asia, Europe, and North America as well as at Larung Gar. Khenpo has taught and translated the Dharma for over thirty years and has lectured on Buddhism and social issues in over a hundred universities around the world. He is one of the leading scholars at Larung Gar and has popularized Tibetan Buddhism among Han Chinese students with numerous bestselling books.

What to Read Next from Wisdom Publications

Tales for Transforming Adversity
A Buddhist Lama's Advice for Life's Ups and Downs
Khenpo Sodargye

One of the world's most popular Tibetan lamas shares accessible advice for working with adversity and living a spiritual life.

The Path
A Guide to Happiness
Khenpo Sherab Zangpo

Khenpo Sherab Zangpo draws on Tibetan Buddhist tradition and his own fascinating life story to describe a way forward for contemporary practitioners, offering lucid guidance on daily practice, finding the right teacher, and cultivating a wiser and more compassionate attitude toward others and ourselves.

Vajrasattva Meditation
An Illustrated Guide
Khenpo Yeshe Phuntsok

Walk step by step through the stages of this tantric ritual of purification with inspired commentary and full-color illustrations.

About Wisdom Publications

Wisdom Publications is the leading publisher of classic and contemporary Buddhist books and practical works on mindfulness. To learn more about us or to explore our other books, please visit our website at wisdompubs.org or contact us at the address below.

Wisdom Publications
199 Elm Street
Somerville, MA 02144 USA

We are a 501(c)(3) organization, and donations in support of our mission are tax deductible.

Wisdom Publications is affiliated with the Foundation for the Preservation of the Mahayana Tradition (FPMT).